STEAK
REVOLUTION

STEAK RE

Collins

VOLUTION

ALL CUTS, ALL WAYS— PERFECT EVERY TIME

ROB FIRING

FOREWORD BY PETER SANAGAN

Steak Revolution
Text copyright © 2018 by Rob Firing.
Foreword copyright © 2018 by Peter Sanagan.
Photographs copyright © 2018 by Rob Firing except for the following:
pp. viii by David Cooper; p. 2 by Scott James; p. 6 by Getty Images; pp. 21 and 177 by iStockphoto.com;
p. 27 from the Library of Congress (item 2007663524); pp. 15, 19, 52-53, 64, 108, 112, 119, 156, 166-167,
175, 178, 181, 186, 189, 195, 202, 206, 209, 210, and 213 by Mike McColl, with styling by Mia Bachmaier;
p. 244 by Noelle Zitzer. Line art on pp. 11 and 16-17 by Nick Craine.

Published by Collins, an imprint of HarperCollins Publishers Ltd

First edition

HarperCollins books may be purchased for educational, business,
or sales promotional use through our Special Markets Department.

HarperCollins Publishers Ltd
2 Bloor Street East, 20th Floor
Toronto, Ontario, Canada
M4W 1A8

www.harpercollins.ca

Library and Archives Canada Cataloguing
in Publication information available upon request.

ISBN 978-1-44345-184-0

Printed and bound in China
RRD/SCP 9 8 7 6 5 4 3 2 1

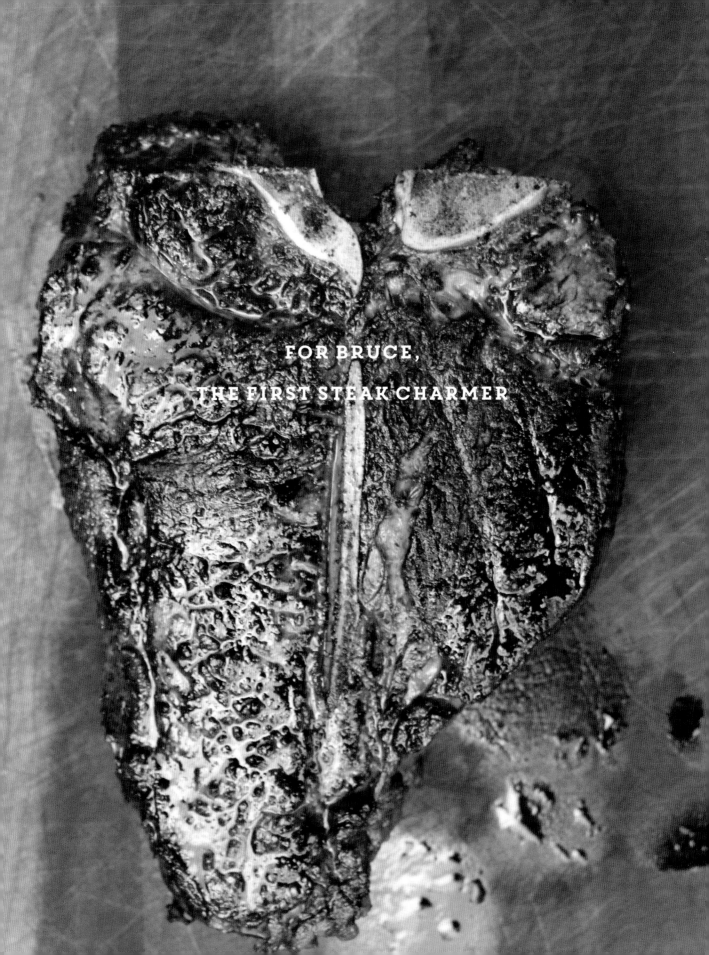

FOR BRUCE,

THE FIRST STEAK CHARMER

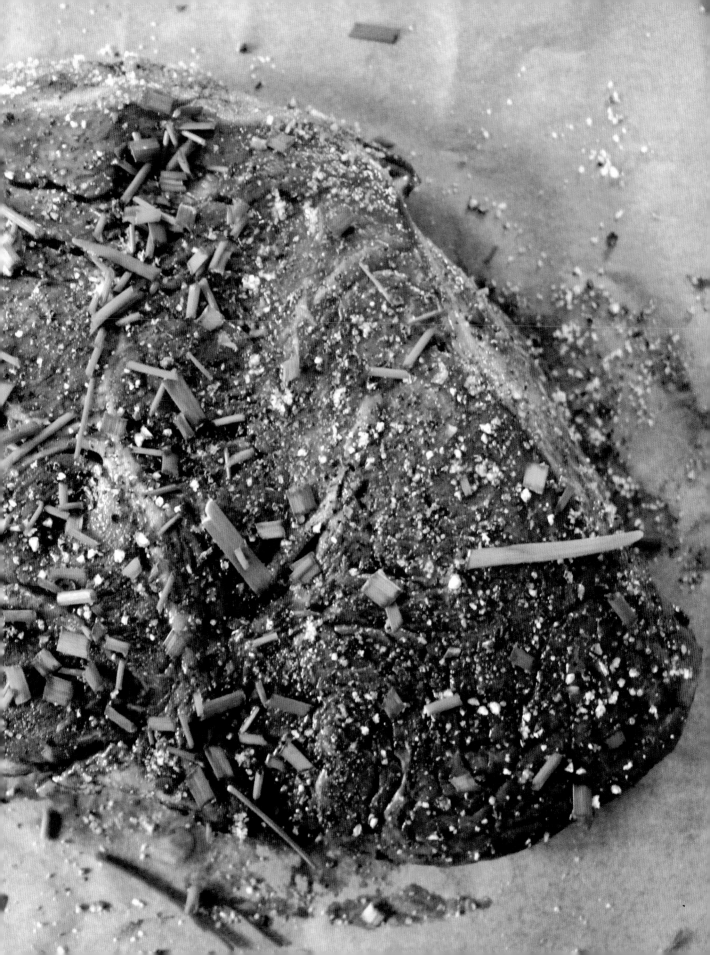

CONTENTS

Peter Sanagan in his butcher shop, Sanagan's Meat Locker,
in Toronto's Kensington Market.

FOREWORD

WHEN I STARTED WORKING IN RESTAURANT KITCHENS, I ALWAYS LOOKED UP TO THE GRILL COOKS. THAT WASN'T JUST BECAUSE I WAS SITTING IN A CORNER, PEELING POTATOES, WHILE THEY LITERALLY TOWERED OVER ME. EVERYONE KNEW THEY WERE THE MOST IMPORTANT COOKS IN THE KITCHEN. THEY MOVED WITH A SENSE OF PURPOSE DURING PREP HOURS: BONING OUT CHICKENS, MARINATING DUCKS, CLEANING BEEF TENDERLOIN AND TRIMMING IT INTO MEDALLIONS. DURING SERVICE IT WAS EVEN BETTER. WATCHING THE DANCE OF AN EXPERIENCED GRILL COOK SHOULD BE AN OLYMPIC SPECTATOR EVENT.

What a lot of diners misunderstand about restaurants is that it is not the chef who controls the flow of the service. It's the grill cook. The chef can get angry and yell and push the grill cook to move faster, but meat cooks in the amount of time meat needs to cook, and no one can change those laws of kitchen physics (I know there are some tricks out there that include the use of salamander broilers and deep-fryers, but I'm talking about proper cooking). Watching an experienced cook command a grill is exciting and akin to watching acrobats—they know just how important their job is to the 200-plus customers who are waiting to be indulged. They nail colour after colour and, just when you think they don't have any steam left, say two hours deep, they chug a bottle of water and keep nailing colours. It's a beautiful thing.

I would watch as the grill cook would stand at the station like a coiled cobra, tongs in hand, just waiting for instruction from the chef. The chef, who was expediting the service, would bark, "Two striploin, one medium, one black and blue! One rib steak, mid-rare! One tenderloin, well done!" "*Oui*, chef!" returned the grill cook, and off they'd go, pulling the protein out of the low-boy line fridge and placing it on the seasoning tray, where it would be snowed with kosher salt and dashed with pepper that had been ground just before service. Then the meat would get a drizzle of olive oil before hitting the hottest spot on the grill. The cook would know just how long that cut needed to sit there before being rotated (if using a traditional grate grill) or, in my case, flipped over on the flat-top griddle. Grill cooks poke and feel the steak for doneness throughout cooking. The more experienced cooks only need to check the meat a couple of times, and then, at the right time, take the steak off the grill to rest. Five or ten minutes later, the steak is ready to go to the pass for the chef to garnish.

I eventually advanced through the kitchen to become a grill cook, and that's when I truly fell in love with meat. That part of my life was what birthed my desire to do what I do today. I really love meat. I love sourcing it; I love cutting it; I love cooking it—and I really love eating it. And in the hierarchy of meat I would have to say that beef (and specifically steak) is right on top. From iron-y flank and hanger to a succulent dry-aged rib steak, not much excites me in the same way. I love talking about steak, and when butchers talk about steak the level of passion is second to none. Except perhaps the passion for steak that Rob Firing has.

Rob has been a customer of Sanagan's since I had my first wee shop back in 2009. He has run through the gamut of cuts from our shop, even having a chicken or two along the way. I remember when Rob and I sat down for a beer about a year ago, and he first revealed his idea for this book. We nerdily talked about steak for an hour or so, and he revealed one of his favourite methods for grilling picanha. Picanha is the top sirloin cap muscle with the fat cap left on. It is a popular Brazilian cut, often seen curled and skewered at rodízio restaurants. Rob described how he would score the fat before marinating, and described the exact timing on the charcoal grill to both render

the fat and make it a delicious part of the eating experience. He couldn't wait to share that recipe with the world, and I understand why. When people truly love something, sometimes the only way of satisfying that love is by sharing it and making it part of other people's lives. I believe that's what Rob has done here, and I hope his infectious passion for steak makes you want to run to your local butcher shop, talk to your butcher about an interesting cut, and then go home and feed yourself, your family, your friends. That's exactly what I'm going to do.

Peter Sanagan
Sanagan's Meat Locker

INTRODUCTION

"WHY DON'T YOU COME OVER TO MY PLACE AND I'LL COOK YOU A STEAK?"

It's a tempting proposition for many of us, powered almost entirely by its last word. Try replacing steak with another perfectly good food: salmon, stir-fry, stew, omelet. It doesn't feel the same. I wouldn't be ungrateful for the offer of a home-cooked stew, but it would hardly be the cure for my broken heart.

There is something particularly special about steak that raises it above the ordinary to among the ranks of indulgences, rewards, and celebrations. Is it because it is expensive or unusually hard to cook? Is it exceptionally rare, or naughty? I think some of these reasons are partly true, but mostly it comes down to our senses.

A properly cooked steak is immensely satisfying, capturing your attention completely. The tongue tastes, the mouth feels and remembers. Teeth carve and bite, and the aromas of dozens of compounds intermingle and delight. Even the sound of a steak on the grill is something to stop and listen to, as dinner guests pause their conversations at the crackle and sizzle, watching the smoke and waiting for its scent.

In *Steak Revolution*, I have tried to give you the richest, most detailed picture possible of this subject. I include what I think a steak is, how other cultures handle steaks, as well as a little about the story of beef, of cows, and of cattle farming. I take care to explain what I've learned over my many years cooking steaks for my friends and family, and in restaurants—techniques for reliable results, and the physics behind those results—to give you full control so you can be a confident steak cook.

There is some philosophizing here, too. I don't linger quite as long on the more expensive and, I think, far too common cuts like striploin, filet mignon, and rib eye, and instead focus on the "butcher's" cuts and sub-primal cuts from other parts of the beast. My reasoning is that this leads us to think of the whole animal and, to a certain degree, the animal itself. As it turns out, these cuts of steak are just as tempting, often more so, than the standard fare on restaurant menus or in supermarkets, and they are almost always dramatically more affordable.

My approach also emphasizes that different cuts of steak are truly different, and benefit from particular cooking methods. The one thing all cuts of steak share, though, is that they require your attention. Steak needs to be watched, and the watching is part of the experience. I doubt there is any other type of cooking more pleasurable than tending a steak over embers, fire, or hot metal, gauging its doneness, urging it along, studying its time on the fire.

For many of you, reading this book will be a journey of discovery. We'll sample the delights of more than a dozen different cuts of steak, each not only remarkably distinct in terms of flavour and structure, but also in how it can be served. All of them vying to be your undeniable favourite. We will create the most fitting accompaniments to steak, inspired by different steak-loving cuisines: pan sauces, raw sauces, reduction sauces; proper, winning salads; and some brilliant ways to cook roots, vegetables, and grains—all of them natural steak partners. I've even included some of my most adored après-steak desserts, the sort of denouement that lets you remember the meal that came before it.

For other readers, those who have already harnessed the magic of the flat iron and culotte, *Steak Revolution* is a hundred visits to different times and places and memories of chefs and steak enthusiasts. It is my clear position regarding some old steak arguments, and a foray into some newer ideas.

In the end, for the novice and veteran steak charmer alike, you will see steak as I have seen it: honestly, respectfully, and, let's face it, greedily. There is no way to hide a steak poorly cooked. There is no way to cook a steak properly without giving it your undivided attention. And there is no way to deny yourself a big, juicy steak done just right.

A STEAK MANIFESTO

EVERYONE CAN MAKE THE PERFECT STEAK

COOKED RIGHT AND SLICED RIGHT, ALL STEAKS ARE TENDER

When cooked to medium-rare, there is hardly such a thing as a tough steak, only a poorly carved one.

EXPENSIVE CUTS ARE NOT ALWAYS THE BEST

Striploin and tenderloin are great, but many other cuts are just as tasty and can be much less expensive. The cow is a very large beast. Why not try the rest of it?

EMBRACE THE FAT

The fat you see in steak is tasty, but the fat you can't see is what gives it flavour.

"TRUST THE SALT"

An Argentine steak proverb. Generously salt your steak before cooking it.

MOVE PAST GRILL MARKS

If you've achieved perfect crosshatched grill marks on your steak, you've missed the point. A nicely developed dark crust changes everything.

BE A STEAK CHARMER

If you give your steak your undivided attention, there is no bad way to cook it.

PART ONE

STEAK
ESSENTIALS

THE FIRST STEAK

AUROCHS, COWS, AND THE ORIGINS OF STEAK

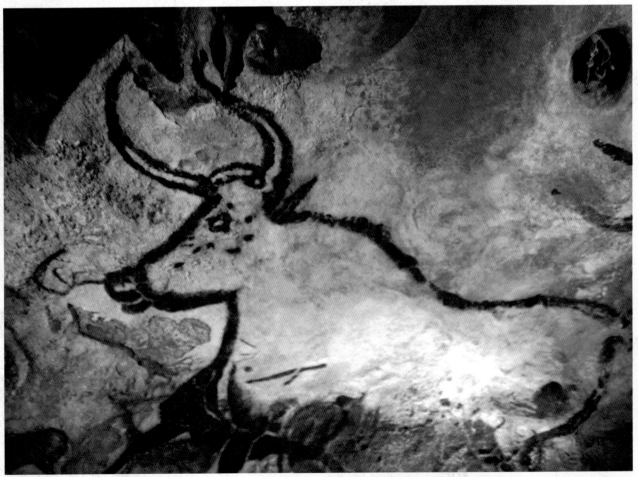

Painting found in the Lascaux caves in the southwest of France, dating back about 17,300 years, depicting the ancestor of the modern cow, the aurochs (*Bos primigenius*).

ore than 15,000 years before the best steakhouses opened in New York and Chicago, Paleolithic humans were busy decorating the walls of their caves with images of their most prized food: the aurochs. A large, long-horned ungulate, the aurochs is the wild ancestor to the modern cow. Interestingly, drawings on the walls of the Lascaux caves in France dating back more than 17,000 years depict the aurochs more prominently than any other animal.

The Lascaux caves are located in Nouvelle-Aquitaine, the same region that gave rise to the famed Limousin breed of cattle, which resembles the aurochs more closely than other breeds. (This is a coincidence, since the domestic cattle in Europe—and North America—today are the descendants of domesticated aurochs of the Near East, which originated roughly 8,000 years ago).

The eventual demise of the aurochs, which shared the same fate as a lot of other Eurasian megafauna, was partly a result of habitat destruction for agriculture, but it was also certainly because aurochs were terrific meat animals. As Mark Schatzker put it so perfectly in his 2010 food chronicle extraordinaire, *Steak: One Man's Search for the World's Tastiest Piece of Beef*: "The wild aurochs, forever extinguished, was cursed by a characteristic that proved to be its undoing: it was delicious."

The beef cattle that were eventually bred from aurochs are large, and have a relatively high meat-to-carcass ratio, just as the aurochs did. This ratio is often called a "dressing percentage"—the amount of meat and bones left on a carcass once the hide, hooves, head, and most organs are removed. It is calculated by dividing the weight of the carcass by the weight of the animal when it was alive, then multiplying it by 100 to express a percentage. Limousin beef, for instance, has a rather high dressing percentage of 63%. Compare that to lambs and goats, which have an average dressing percentage of 50%.

The aurochs's high ratio of meat may have been the evolutionary outcome of its extraordinary capacity to break down tremendous quantities of grass into sugars, proteins, and other nutrients (it also made them relatively safe from many predators). This means that farmers and hunters could carve these animals into large pieces, delineated by major parts of their bodies, and then into many smaller pieces, defined against other natural boundaries like bones and adjacent muscle groups. The word "steak" is actually derived from the Old Norse word *stykki* or "piece."

As dairy cows and beef cattle were being raised on pasture previously the domain of aurochs and other grazers, aurochs took refuge in increasingly marginal habitats, including wooded floodplains and marshland. This is something of a sad irony, since their extinction coincided with the advent of their genetic extension, *Bos taurus*, the domesticated cattle now numbering over one billion worldwide (and one for every three people in North America). One might imagine some of the last remaining aurochs meeting eyes with their significantly smaller domesticized descendants grazing on pasture that was once theirs—*Bos taurus* surging in their numbers, while *Bos primigenius* dwindled to dangerous lows.

The aurochs became extinct in Central Europe in the 1620s. It has been documented that the last remaining animal, a female, died in the Jaktorów woods in Masovia, in central east Poland, in 1627.

THE MODERN COW

The beef that many of us eat today is dramatically different from that of our ancestors, and it's not merely because the cows themselves have changed. Rather, it's the cows' diets. As the aurochs were before them, cows are adapted specifically to eat grass as the principal component of their diet (instead of high-energy feeds like corn). The importance of this is not marginal, and the effects of changing the diet of an animal so specialized has dramatic outcomes for the overall health of the animal and the resulting chemistry of its meat.

Cows and many other grazers, like goats, sheep, deer, giraffes, and moose, are equipped with rumen, and are classified as ruminants, which is a suborder of the hoofed beasts known generally as ungulates. A rumen is like a stomach in that it performs a key function in the initial breakdown of food into constituent nutrients, but unlike a stomach in other ways. While the single-chambered stomachs of other mammals such as cats, pigs, and humans act on food by containing it and exposing it to acids and enzymes, rumen are in essence incubating chambers for microbes, which perform the essential task of breaking down otherwise indigestible cellulose—the principal carbohydrate in grasses—into simpler sugars.

These sugars in turn not only feed the cow but also feed the microbes at various stages of pre-stomach digestion. Cows have three pre-stomach chambers (the rumen, reticulum, and omasum) and one "true" stomach (the abomasum). Each pre-stomach chamber contains specialized environments suitable to and in part created by the lifestyles of various types of bacteria, protists (single-celled life forms that can propel themselves in their environments), and fungi. Cows don't just digest plant material, they ferment it.

It is remarkable how much protein the body of a cow manufactures simply from digesting grass, although it isn't quite as simple as that. Most of the protein is derived not from the grass itself but from protists that thrive in the rumen, as well as bacteria. After these microbes are done breaking down cellulose in the rumen and reticulum, they are flushed into the cow's abomasum, where they are exposed to hydrochloric acid, broken down, and then absorbed as amino acids, the building blocks of protein.

Bacteria, protozoa, and fungi operate symbiotically to produce food for each other and for the cow, converting cellulose to other sugars, and sugars to starches and fatty acids. Fatty acids produce enzymes, making nutrients bio-available and creating other by-products in the process. One of these by-products is hydrogen, which in turn is consumed by a group of bacteria, called methanogens, which produce methane. (Up to 60% of the methane produced in general by agricultural activities is from burping or farting ruminants, and most of that—just under 56 million metric tons in a year—is from cows. Methane is a powerful greenhouse gas, and cows, along with farm animals generally, have been the subject of debate among those interested in mitigating climate change.)

Cows with healthy microbial cultures in their rumen and reticulum will actually burp methane. Cows with imbalanced rumen—those raised primarily on corn, or finished too long on corn or other concentrated feed—will produce methane, too, but at the other end of their digestive tracts, along with elevated levels of *E. coli* bacteria, which can infect beef products during processing.

What a cow eats determines how effectively the highly evolved digestive system operates, setting the microbial population balance and resulting chemistry of the animal's tissues. Experienced cattle farmers know that if they want to "finish" a cow on concentrated feed—fattening it with grains or other high-energy foods before slaughter—they must do this gradually, allowing the animal and its complement of microbes to adjust from a diet of grass to the much starchier feed, and that they must not keep their cattle on this diet for too long.

By comparison, cows raised on grass or "forage," which also contains legumes and other plants (but still mostly grass, and sometimes partly fermented or "pickled" grass, or silage), accumulate polyunsaturated body fat deposits with a much lower omega-6 (linoleic acid) to omega-3 (alpha-linolenic acid) ratio: 3:1. The ratio for cows fed on concentrated feeds like corn is up to 20:1. (To put it into perspective, wild coldwater fish like salmon have a fat profile with an omega-6 to omega-3 ratio of about 1:10. Farmed salmon have a ratio of 1:3. Hydrogenated oils like margarine [from soy] have a ratio of 7:1. Processed sunflower oil has a ratio of 70:1.)

Humans cannot synthesize either of these essential fatty acids, so must acquire them at appropriate levels in their diets. Unfortunately, the appropriate ratio that humans evolved to ingest is 1:1, which is exactly the ratio found in cuisines of wild or traditionally raised foods, and an increasingly rare ratio found in modern ingredients.

Grass-fed cows also have significantly higher concentrations of conjugated linoleic acid (CLA) in their fat. The consumption of CLA has been the subject of many studies linking it to healthy long-term weight levels and resistance to certain cancers. CLA is not synthesized per se by cows, but produced by microbes in healthy rumens.

There are many reasons to be concerned about how cattle are raised and in particular about what they eat—from a nutritional standpoint (for the cow and for the cow eater), from an environmental standpoint, and from the standpoint that we're focusing on here: how beef tastes and behaves when it comes time to cook and eat it.

A COW'S LIFE

Most beef cattle in North America are slaughtered at two years of age, at the most, and the sad fact of the matter is that a lot of those animals live less than healthy lives in crowded, artificial conditions. This almost always means the animals damage rather than improve the land on which they live. They also require a host of external inputs like food and water, growth hormones, and antibiotics, not to mention chemical fertilizer and land-clearing to grow their feed. However, an increasing number of ranchers and dairy farmers have come to understand that raising cows in a manner that is more in tune with nature brings many environmental services and economic benefits, as well as vastly improves the health and welfare of the animals. These happier and healthier animals result in a product that provides superior nutrition for those of us who consume their meat and milk.

The figure on page 11 illustrates how some enlightened ranchers are now raising cattle. In a sense it is a step backward: it resembles practices that were employed by farmers for hundreds of years. In the grand scheme of things, though, it is of course a huge step in the right direction. With some key advances in modern science and technology, ranchers can now closely mimic the forces of nature that created the natural landscapes upon which animals like cows (or more precisely, their ancestors) and humans evolved.

Consensus within the beef industry on the best way to raise cattle is still a long way off, but some revolutionaries are leading the way. For example, see rancher Nicolette Hahn Niman's excellent book *Defending Beef* (Chelsea Green, 2014) for a survey of North American beef industry practices and a convincing debunking of some unfortunate misconceptions about beef. I consider her family's ranch in California an ideal model for most cattle-dense regions in North America. If you're interested in knowing more about the health and environmental benefits of naturally raised cattle, take a look at Graham Harvey's book *Grass-Fed Nation* (Icon Books, 2016).

COWS AND METHANE

Contrary to popular belief, most cows are not a major source of excess atmospheric carbon or methane. Cows, properly raised the way nature intended (as opposed to industrially raised, which certainly does cause problems), perform important environmental services, just like the billions of mega-grazers did before humans denuded the earth of most of them. The total number of cows on the planet right now is but a fraction of the gigantic herds of grazing animals that existed 15,000 years ago, before humans began hunting them in earnest.

Properly grazed land helps poor soil recover its physical and biological properties lost due to modern farming practices. Water retention increases, as does soil fertility and the soil's ability to sequester and hold carbon from the atmosphere, and soil erosion and desertification decrease. Cows and other large grazers, once kings of their domain, have been a natural part of the carbon and methane cycle for more than 50 million years.

BETTER BEEF
RAISING CATTLE THE RIGHT WAY

1. A calf is born and nurses from its mother, who grazes on pasture. This ensures that the calf receives a nutritionally balanced diet with all the inoculatory benefits, which are of particular importance to an animal that uses microbes to the degree that a cow does to digest its food. After approximately six months, the calf will have been naturally weaned to a diet of grass and pasture vegetation, joining the herd as they graze on seasonal pasture.

2. Ideally, herds are of a density appropriate to the land they graze, mimicking the numbers that would occur in nature (wild grazers compete for food and gather in tight formations to discourage predators). Cattle are periodically encouraged to move to new pasture when the vegetation has been eaten roughly halfway down, as would happen if predators were patrolling their perimeters and harassing the herd. This movement has a huge effect on the vegetation dynamics in the pasture, generally fostering the growth of grasses over other plants, exposing the growth points of the plants to the sun, embedding seeds and dead vegetation in the soil with the herd's heavy hooves, and fertilizing the land with manure and urine. This is sometimes called "paddock grazing" or "rotational grazing."

3. As the calf and herd mature, the soil under the pasture accumulates organic material, attains crucial fungal balances, retains much more water, becomes looser and loamy, sequesters carbon, encourages a more natural ecosystem, and attracts more native animals to populate it, improving biodiversity.

As cows remain on pasture in appropriate numbers and are moved at the right times to new, adjacent ground, they stay healthy. So, too, does the land, resisting the forces of erosion as the soil improves and as the roots of grasses and flowering plants form long networks below, often far greater in length than the plants above ground. The methane that cows produce from burping (because they employ bacterial methanogens as part of their gut flora) is in turn consumed by naturally occurring bacterial methanotrophs at ground level, where the cows' mouths are most of the time. Since some of the grass they eat would have rotted on the ground and converted to methane in any case, the methane cycle is naturally balanced on healthy pasture land.

4. After five years, the cow is ready for slaughter. Ideally, this takes place on the farm property itself, avoiding added stress on the animal and the costs of fuel that transportation would entail. The meat is denser and somewhat darker in colour, as well as nutritionally superior. This includes the fat, which has a much healthier omega-3 to omega-6 fatty acid balance, and takes on a yellow hue from high levels of carotenoids accumulated from a life of eating grass.

5. If the cow is actually a cow (as opposed to a steer, which is a castrated male), and one of the fittest in the herd, she will be inseminated, and the cycle begins anew.

1.

Calf remains with mother, joining the larger herd at six months of age.

2.

Calves are densely packed and moved to new pasture frequently, mimicking natural predator and feeding dynamics.

3.

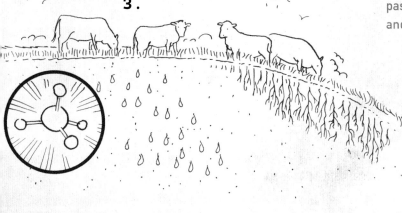

Grazing cows improve soil biology over time and sequester carbon in the soil. As soil improves, it retains more water, reducing erosion and runoffs, making surface water clearer. Ecosystem is normalized, native species benefit, and pasture becomes methane-balanced.

4.

At five years of age, the majority of the cows are slaughtered onsite, which is better for the animals' welfare than transporting them elsewhere. The nutrient value of the meat is optimal, as a result of a natural diet.

5.

Cows with the most desirable characteristics live to breed again, improving the herd.

GRASS-FED VS. GRAIN-FED

Let's compare steaks from grass-fed cows—the most similar to those eaten by our ancestors—to steaks from cows raised on increasing levels of corn or other grains. The first thing you will notice in grass-fed beef, besides the higher price tag, is that it is significantly less marbled with fat. Grass-fed beef raised on pasture has a completely different fat profile, and less fat in general. This is due, in part, to several factors: the cows had time to properly ruminate their food, the cows got a lot more exercise, and compared with corn and other grains (or other finishing feeds, which can include beets, molasses, potatoes, crop by-products, soy products, animal rendering and other animal by-products, and even post-retail candy), grass is simply a lower-energy food, less quickly digested.

It's not like there is no fat in grass-fed beef—cuts near the ribs and loin are still relatively fatty—but the interstitial fat (as opposed to the "visceral" clumps of fat) otherwise known as marbling is dramatically reduced overall. This affects not only the taste of the meat when it's cooked, but also the rate at which it loses moisture, the cooking time, the overall texture and mouthfeel of the meat, and the extent to which it will brown and form a crust without something to help it along. (See discussion of Maillard reaction on page 23.)

What you might notice next about grass-fed beef is the colour, which tends to be darker and deeper than grain-fed beef when comparing the same cuts. The reason for this is an increased level of myoglobin, the protein present in muscle tissues that perform sustained, hard work. Myoglobin in muscle tissue, like hemoglobin in blood, binds oxygen to iron, making oxygen readily available to cells. It is flavourful on its own, giving meat an unmistakable ferrous taste, and adds more flavour when it is broken down by heating, when it degrades and gives up some of its iron to the interstitial fat in the meat, causing the fat to oxidize somewhat. There are too many flavour-producing reactions going on to explain right here, but we'll get to this soon.

Finally, you will notice the colour of the visceral fat: the fat caps on the edges of certain cuts like striploin and prime rib, and the clumps of fat in fattier cuts. Cows raised on pasture, or mostly pasture, that eat grass for nearly their whole lives will produce meat with somewhat yellowish fat. This is because of the increased levels of carotenoids—the precursors of vitamin A—they ingest in their diet.

There are good arguments in support of both exclusively grass-fed (pasture-raised) beef and for beef that is lightly finished on natural feed, like whole grains. As for grain-fed beef or beef raised on other concentrated feed products for too long—sometimes for several months, which usually means the cows are raised in abhorrent, crowded conditions and are exposed to pathogens, necessitating regimens of powerful antibiotics and nutritional supplements—I would just avoid it altogether. When raised properly and humanely, cattle have a role in sustainable modern agriculture, especially when the meat they produce is regarded as it should be: a special treat to be lovingly prepared and eaten only as often as our best farming practices can sustain.

The first steak, whether cut from an animal that was hunted or raised, was certainly from a grass-fed animal, but since the advent of agriculture, including grain crops, preceded the widespread domestication of *Bos primigenius* by roughly 4,000 years in parts of Europe and Asia, I think it is likely that finishing practices were also used even in the earliest instances of beef husbandry.

The meat of the grass-fed steak shown here is darker than that of conventional steak, reflecting a different protein structure and higher iron levels. The fat is yellower, containing more carotenoids.

I have found references to grain-finished beef versus exclusively pasture-raised beef dating back to the mid-1700s in Britain, though these comparisons were made, at least initially, only to test the costs of producing meat and milk, and had nothing in particular to do with quality. I would hazard a guess that if we searched for reliable references from much earlier times in the Near East, where both wheat and cows came from, we would find that the earliest cattle herders sometimes finished cows on grain, too.

By the time steak cuisine had matured to the point where different parts of the cow were being sold for different prices, cuisines from regions around the world, from Europe to Japan, Australia to North and South America, had developed their own names for steaks, their own ways of parsing the animal, their own favourite cooking techniques, their own ways of raising cattle, and their own breeds of *Bos taurus* (and *Bos indicus*, the Eastern cousin).

I have come to the conclusion, many, many steaks later, that the particular breed of cow has much less to do with how a steak tastes and performs than one might infer from so much attention paid to heirloom breeds like Black Angus and Wagyu. Determining what makes a good piece of meat has far more to do with how the individual live animal was treated and what it ate. So, for the most part, in this book I steer clear of getting into the merits and history of cattle breeds. Most of the differences among the various breeds have more to do with the shape of the animal, its growth rate, and how the live animal behaves than anything else, and is more relevant to the farmer and the butcher than the steak eater.

HOW TO BUY STEAK

THOUGHTFUL BUTCHERS, CARING FARMERS

Since in this book I'm focusing on the butchers' cuts of steak instead of the ubiquitous (though also delicious) striploin, rib eye, and filet mignon, I will refer you to a butcher shop when it comes time to acquire a decent piece of meat, although I will concede that there have been tremendous improvements in some grocery stores that have reacted to the growing segment of consumers interested in higher-quality meat.

The new jargon associated with a wide range of foods can be overwhelming and sometimes even misleading. For example, you can choose between free-range, free-run, organic, or cage-free chickens and eggs. Or pasture-raised and heritage pork. Or grass-fed, high-protein, or organic milk. Beef has not been spared the confusion.

The retail categories for beef, which already had its own unique industry "grade" categories, ostensibly for fattiness (Prime, Choice, Select, and Standard in the United States, and AAA, AA, and A in Canada), have bloomed into a dazzling bouquet of terminology. Where all a consumer needed to care about 30 years ago was whether their beef was lean or extra lean (or not lean at all), these days a steak might be labelled organic or naturally raised, grass-fed, corn-fed, hormone- and antibiotic-free, or farm-raised. It could also be designated by where the animal was raised ("Ontario beef" or "Florida beef"), as well as the breed of cow (Black Angus, Wagyu, or Limousin) and the degree and method of aging (wet or dry aged, 26 days, 40 days, and so on).

The grading systems for beef in North America and elsewhere are actually derived from amalgamating formulas informed by how old an animal is, how fat it is, and how that fat is distributed within the beast. These systems are remarkably complicated, and at the same time incomplete, in my view. If you're interested, see the USDA charts and formulas on offer from Texas A&M University (https://meat.tamu.edu/beefgrading/).

Whether you're shopping at a major retailer or a local butcher shop, at some point you are going to have to inform yourself of your options and, to some extent, take a leap of faith and trust the person who is selling you your steak. Ask questions. Better butchers are generally delighted to engage. Your butcher should know which farms their meat comes from, where the animal was slaughtered, and how the animal was raised and fed. A lot of the time butchers will have a direct relationship with the cattle farmer, having chosen to buy their beef from a particular farm because they appreciate how well the animals are raised and know that it's reflected in the quality of the meat.

I have visited many beef farms over the years, but frankly most people will never make it to the farm that raised the cow that ended up in their favourite butcher shop or see firsthand the conditions under which an animal was raised. The confidence you have in your butcher takes care of this missing link.

Only after you've done your homework will you be able to buy a steak that will blow your mind and the minds of your dinner guests.

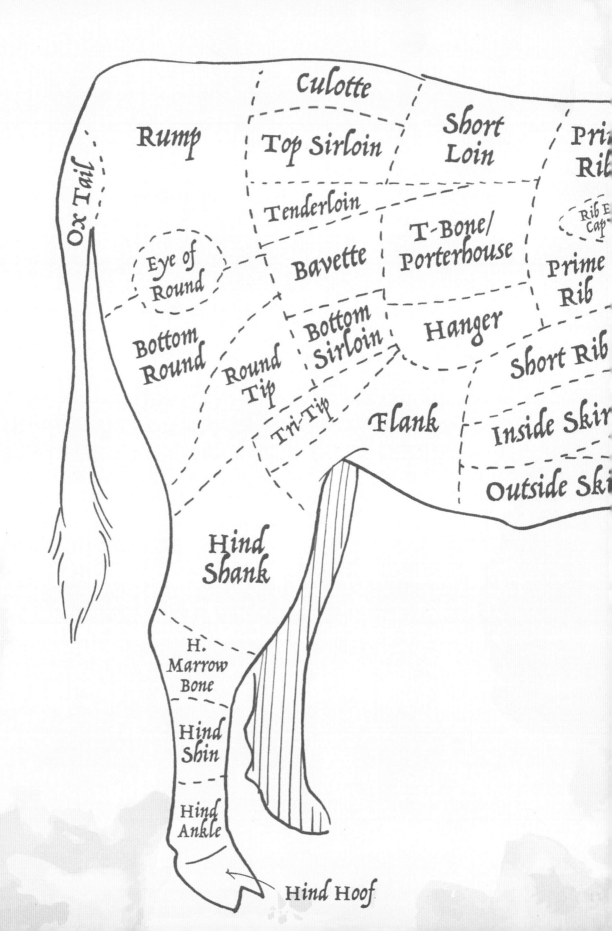

Culotte

Rump

Top Sirloin

Short Loin

Pri Ri

Ox Tail

Tenderloin

Rib E Cap

Eye of Round

Bavette

T-Bone/ Porterhouse

Prime Rib

Bottom Round

Bottom Sirloin

Hanger

Round Tip

Short Rib

Tri Tip

Flank

Inside Skir

Outside Ski

Hind Shank

H. Marrow Bone

Hind Shin

Hind Ankle

Hind Hoof

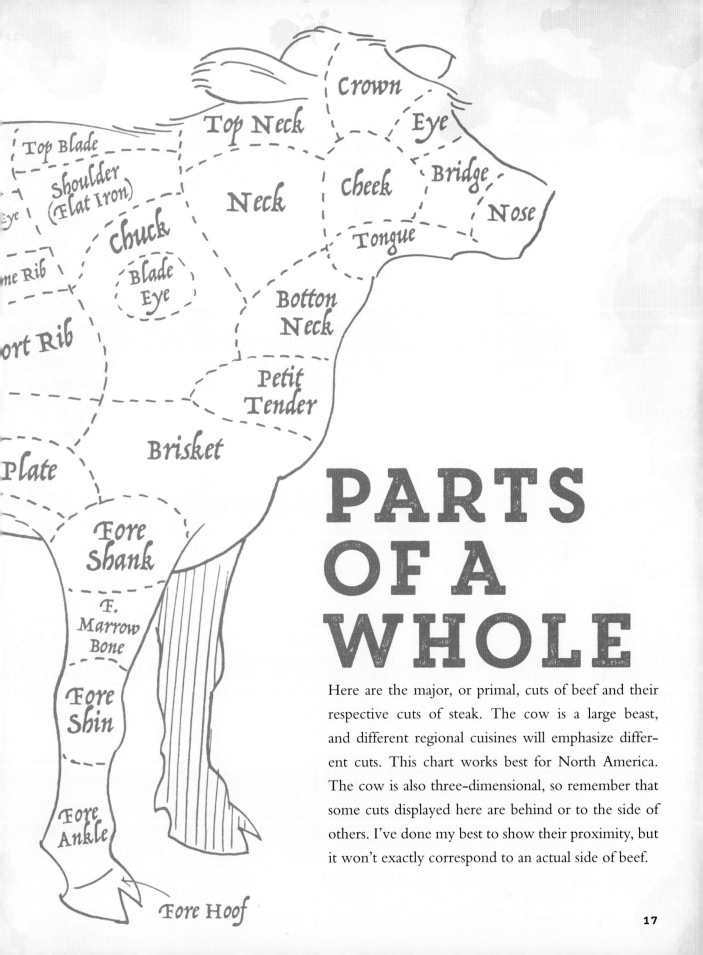

Top Blade

Shoulder
(Flat Iron)

...Eye

Chuck

Blade
Eye

...me Rib

...ort Rib

Top Neck

Neck

Crown

Eye

Cheek

Bridge

Nose

Tongue

Botton
Neck

Petit
Tender

Brisket

...Plate

Fore
Shank

F.
Marrow
Bone

Fore
Shin

Fore
Ankle

Fore Hoof

PARTS OF A WHOLE

Here are the major, or primal, cuts of beef and their respective cuts of steak. The cow is a large beast, and different regional cuisines will emphasize different cuts. This chart works best for North America. The cow is also three-dimensional, so remember that some cuts displayed here are behind or to the side of others. I've done my best to show their proximity, but it won't exactly correspond to an actual side of beef.

HOW A GREAT STEAK LOOKS (AND SMELLS) IN THE RAW

I distinctly remember returning from market shopping one afternoon a few years back with a box of greens and potatoes, and a rather gigantic slice of a whole sirloin wrapped in brown paper, from one of my favourite butcher shops. After opening the package and gazing at what I imagined would soon be a steak dinner for the history books, I couldn't help but give it a sniff. The meat smelled fresh and ferrous, and the thick cap of fat smelled sweet and creamy.

Though it is generally not acceptable to sniff your meat before buying it, the way a piece of meat smells is important. Of course, looks are important, too. Deliberately aged steaks will look and smell significantly different than younger steaks.

All beef is aged to a certain extent, with whole sides and quarters hung in a refrigerated environment for about 7 days from the moment the animal is slaughtered and processed. Beef is then aged "wet" (vacuum sealed and refrigerated in heavy plastic bags) or "dry" (left open to the air, ideally refrigerated at 40°F).

DRY-AGED STEAK

Dry-aged steak is hung in a refrigerated environment for anywhere up to 60 days, but generally between 28 and 40 days. It loses up to 30% of its weight through moisture loss, which is the primary reason for its higher price tag. As it spends weeks in the counterintuitively named "hotbox" (a climate-controlled fridge), care is taken to carve off and discard the outer layers (another reason for its high price tag), which have inevitably decayed. The result is a steak that is more distinctly flavoured, more tender, and more finely textured. Dry-aged steaks can have an almost nutty taste with hints of cheese. When cooked, they reach doneness more quickly than normally aged steaks, and have a more even, less resistant bite.

You will notice that dry-aged steaks are darker, more rigid, and drier-looking, with less sheen, and are sometimes a bit smaller than their normally aged counterparts of the same cut. To the novice, they may look dirtier, but all things equal, they are most certainly not. Dry-aged steaks are not as juicy as normally aged (wet-aged) steaks. Different rules apply, and we will get into these delicious particulars in the chapters to come.

NORMALLY AGED (WET-AGED) STEAK

Normally-aged steak is generally cut into sides or quarters and hung for a week in a refrigerated environment after the animal is slaughtered. Primal cuts—the first, larger cuts of beef before they are further broken down into sub-primal cuts, and then retail cuts (steaks,

In contrast to how most steaks are aged, the meat of a dry-aged steak is drier and darker, and the fat more compressed and desiccated. Dry-aged steaks have more concentrated flavours and different flavour compounds, and are always more expensive than their younger fellows.

ARTISAN J .29
27.27.KG

brisket, roasts, on so on)—can be wet aged in high-grade vacuum-packed plastic bags for up to three weeks. They make up the vast majority of meat sold to consumers. These steaks should be moist and bright. If they're not, this could be an indication that they have been cut and left out for too long. Myoglobin will oxidize after several hours, essentially rusting. While this isn't necessarily bad for you, too much oxidization can change the taste to something that hints at stale.

When steak is cut, creating more surface area and exposing the meat to the air for the first time, it creates an environment more readily colonized by microbes, especially bacteria. Not all bacteria are bad, but some are. Even if most of the harmful elements can be cooked off the surface of a colonized steak, a severely affected piece of meat can be soured, giving it an off taste. This meat will likely be oxidized already, brown and dull, and can also be tacky. This sticky slime, or "biofilm," is an extracellular substance produced by some kinds of bacteria to protect themselves from microbial competition and to help them reproduce more quickly. (Biofilm of a rather different kind is also what eventually gives foods like yogurt and crème fraîche their structure. Bacteria multiply and create structure to help them in their environments, resulting in a deliberately edible by-product. But that's not what we're talking about here.) Some sliminess is completely natural, and is merely part of the meat itself. Avoid meat that is brown and sticky, accompanied by off smells.

Steaks that have passed their prime, or steaks of poor quality, can be artificially coloured, resulting in an unnatural, uniformly red meat. The practice is base and aims to mislead the consumer. Steaks like this are usually found shrink-wrapped in Styrofoam trays on the shelves of inferior supermarkets. There really is no good way to cook this kind of meat, and because it can be difficult to determine exactly why the meat was altered in the first place, I can't think of a good reason to bother with it.

A good wet-aged steak, or steaks that simply haven't been aged at all after their week of hanging, will taste fresh and tangy, with fat that is rich and sweet. Look for them in a clean butcher's case, with different kinds of meat having some sort of effective separation (pork is set away from chicken, and away from beef). This tells you that your butcher is thinking seriously about the dangers of cross-contamination.

In short, wet-aged meat should smell fresh, and dry-aged meat should smell somewhat richer, but still pleasant. Vinegar or ammonia smells are not good.

Whichever sort of aged steak you choose, be sure to choose it well. Steak is special, and spectacularly good when the farmers and butchers have done their due. Wet- or dry-aged steak is not so much a different quality as it is a matter of taste.

SPANISH COWS

You've heard of aged steak, but how about aged cows? The cows in the Basque Country of northern Spain can be as old as 18 years, and are highly prized for their meat. They are fed only grass from the fertile ranches of the region, with virtually no other inputs. Some Basque ranchers even source dairy cows from other parts of Europe when the cows are "retired" and then give them an additional few years on their pastures. The cows' fat is yellow thanks to the carotenoids (the precursor to vitamin A) that have accumulated over years of eating a grass-only diet, the way cows are supposed to. The meat is really terrific, and steaks in Basque are called *txuleta*, which translates roughly to "chop." I think they are, hands down, the king of steaks, and I just about fainted the first time I tried one. They are cooked on a hot grill over hardwood charcoal with lots of salt, and served along with their yellow fat, which is sometimes cooked separately because it cooks at a different rate. Cattlemen used to trade the meat for *cidre*, which gave rise to the cider-house cuisine famous in the region.

CRUST, FAT, JUICE

THE THREE ELEMENTS OF PERFECT STEAK

That *ahhhh* moment of the first anticipated mouthful of magnificence that is a steak, done just right—what do you notice about it? It's juicy, yes. Appropriately salty. Incomprehensibly savoury. Rich and satisfying. Your mouth and nostrils are lit up with a symphony of flavours that coalesce into something unmistakably wonderful: smokiness, tanginess, hints of caramel, and mouthfeel ranging from velvety to slippery to supple. All accompanied by the voluptuous textures of sweet fat, or the tawny bite of a perfect crust. I contend that only beef steak can deliver this much in one bite, and here you will learn how to create this same experience every time you light the fire, the gas grill, or the stovetop.

Your goal is to cook your steak so that it develops a dark brown crust, so that all the internal fat is melted enough to participate in the overall campaign, and so that the steak juices are released from the muscle fibres but not from the steak itself. There are exceptions, matters of taste, and extra flavours you can add to steak in wonderfully playful ways, but really, once you've mastered this essential goal, the rest takes care of itself. Expressed in just three words: crust, fat, juice.

CRUST

The delectable outer coating of a steak cooked well will pack enough flavour to completely change its character. Part of what gives the crust it's awesome flavour power is the chemical transformation of sugars and proteins as they bond together while cooking. They can only do this fast enough at temperatures in excess of 280°F, which is why steak needs to be cooked, at least for some of its time on the heat, in a dry environment. Otherwise moisture will cool the surface down too much for the reaction to occur on time. The phenomenon is called the "Maillard reaction," named after the French chemist Louis-Camille Maillard, who discovered it in the early 1900s. This reaction occurs with a great many foods: anything that is cooked at high temperatures in a dry environment for long enough (bread, roasted nuts, cookies, coffee beans) or at lower temperatures over very long periods (meat and vegetable stocks cooked for many hours). It is the source of complex networks of dozens of flavour compounds, some of which are fleeting, breaking down or combining to create still other flavour com-

THE SEARING MYTH

I often hear people talk about the importance of "searing in the juices" while cooking a steak. Simply put, searing does no such thing. Some juices will run from your steak no matter what, and searing a crust will not help. As a matter of course, steak will lose up to one-third of its moisture when cooked, even at medium-rare. A steak is 75% water when it's raw. But you needn't worry: the fat inside the steak will guard against a dry, unhappy result. Of some importance, though, is the grain. If the grain runs through the steak from top to bottom (like it does with a New York striploin), cooking will release moisture more quickly than a steak with a grain that runs across its length. It is worth checking doneness on steaks with a vertical grain a little earlier than steaks with horizontal grain.

pounds. The reaction is particularly pronounced in steak because of its rather generous amino-acid profile (it has a lot of protein to work with). The sugar in this protein–sugar partnership is glycogen (sometimes called animal starch), a polysaccharide of glucose that is stored in muscle tissue to fuel the live beast.

The crust is also formed by caramelization, the chemical reaction that occurs when sugar is reduced in a dry environment at temperatures in excess of 230°F (or hotter for some sugars). Like the Maillard reaction, caramelization produces hundreds of flavour compounds, the ultimate stage of which is pyrolysis, or charring. Char, unwelcome most of the time in large quantities, can be part of the flavour profile and texture of nice crust. If a little char can be nice, the rule for crust should always be "brown, not black." When you see the steak fats and juices bubbling on top of the dark brown exterior as you turn the steak, you know your crust has sufficiently developed. If your crust has developed but your steak is not cooked internally to the level you like, this may be the time to move it to a cooler spot until it is.

The Maillard reaction occurs more readily in an alkaline environment, so adding too much acidity to your steak (like a squeeze of lemon) as it cooks will limit browning. Salt is good, though. Regular table salt (sodium chloride) is pH-neutral, but will allow your steak to hold more moisture internally, if you add it early enough before you start cooking. Unrefined sea salts do contain water-reactive minerals, and will in fact raise pH, creating a somewhat more alkaline cooking surface. For this reason, I recommend using the greyish Celtic style of sea salt, or the Himalayan salts, which also contain water-reactive elements.

THE TAKEAWAY FOR GREAT CRUSTS:
Ample heat, limited moisture, a low acid or neutral cooking environment, and meat salted well in advance of cooking (at least 30 minutes, preferably longer— even a day before).

FAT

Yes, you want it. Fat is important enough that beef is actually graded on how much intramuscular fat (marbling) and visceral fat (the larger, visible clusters) any given cut contains. In my view, beef grades should be a bit less fat-based, because real meat quality is much more nuanced than that. But grading has its merits. In Canada, beef grades range from Prime (contains the most marbling), AAA (somewhat less marbling), then AA and A, to four grades each of B, D, and E. In the United States, beef is similarly graded from Prime (very well marbled) to Choice, Select, Standard, Commercial, Utility, Cutter, and finally Canner.

The quantity and distribution of fat is measured along with the age of the cow, with the assumption that younger, fatter cows will yield a superior cooking and eating experience. Meat from younger cows is paler, and generally has a finer texture. The more and better distributed fat is in a younger cow, the higher the rating. Grading systems are similar around the world, with Japan leading the way in the degree of specification, though the age of the cow varies. In Australia and Argentina, beef cattle can be four or five years old. In Spain, Galician cows are raised to be slaughtered much closer to the end of the cow's natural lifespan, approaching 15 years or more. The meat from these Spanish cows is much darker, and the fat much yellower.

THE TRUTH ABOUT FAT

There is so much health mythology about fat that it is hard to know where to begin. Fats are essential to the human diet, and animal fats have been a part of the human diet since humans were human. Saturated fats, which are found in the visceral (triglyceride) fat bodies in steak, remain stable at high temperatures, not only giving them a high smoke point but also preventing them from becoming toxic, as many polyunsaturated vegetable fats do when heated. Unsaturated (vegetable) fats have the molecular capacity to readily bond with other compounds when processed or heated, creating harmful free radicals. For an update on the benefits of this tragically vilified macronutrient, take a look at *The Big Fat Surprise: Why Butter, Meat and Cheese Belong in a Healthy Diet* by Nina Teicholz (Simon & Schuster, 2014).

Lower grades of beef are more likely to have other factors working against them, like inconsistent meat colour, cows that were too old when they were slaughtered, and low muscle density.

Suffice it to say that fat plays an important role. It adds richness to meat, protects it from moisture loss and evens out the heat while it cooks, and generally makes so many aspects of cooking and eating steak much better.

Since the goal is to make the fat in your steak deliciously melty, as opposed to stiff and fudgy, it's important to know that different kinds of fat have different melting points. The more saturated the fat, the higher the melting point. Unsaturated fats have double carbon bonds, causing a bend in the fatty acid chain that makes it harder for them to pack together, and so they become looser and liquefy more quickly as the temperature rises.

Many steak cuts are blanketed in a significant fat layer or cap of hard fat (the fat cap). This mostly saturated fat takes the longest to melt, and will remain largely intact when your steak is done. Generally speaking, the fat cap is best left untrimmed, as it generally is with striploin and some sirloin steaks. This adds another tasty dimension to your steak, so why not take advantage of it? Some of it will darken and char a little on the grill because it is exposed directly to the heat. That just makes things delicious, and in my view more handsome on the plate. Steaks with fat caps are also great to pan-fry. You can use the steak's own fat to coat the bottom of your pan.

As it turns out, the fat that holds moisture inside the meat is quite special. Unlike marbling and visceral fat like fat caps, it is invisible. Also unlike the visible fat, it is largely unsaturated and will melt at lower temperatures, starting around 85°F. These fats, called phospholipids, are an essential component of the cell walls of the live animal, and once they begin melting in earnest in your steak, they release fluids (juice) from the muscle tissue. The trick is to start this process—fracturing the layers between muscle fibres, making the steak juicy—but not overdo it. It's important to leave enough tissue unaffected so as much juicy goodness as possible remains in your steak instead of on your carving board or plate. In my view, this means cooking the steak to an internal temperature of 120°F to 125°F, depending on your cut of meat. The French call this, appropriately, *à point*, signifying that the steak is perfectly cooked. It amounts to a little under medium-rare by North American standards.

This is not to undervalue the visible (triglyceride) fat. It also melts when cooked, trapping moisture, distributing heat more evenly, developing rich flavours, and lubricating your steak into a state of sumptuousness.

THE TAKEAWAY FOR OPTIMAL FATTY GOODNESS: Melt the fat, but not too much. With some exceptions, this generally means removing your steak from the heat as it approaches an internal temperature of 125°F.

JUICE

There is nothing like crushing a nice bite of steak between your molars, brightly flavourful juices gushing from its structure and over your tongue. All the water-soluble flavours, and some of the fat-soluble ones, are contained here in the tangy liquid essence of steak. A steak cooked above medium (135°F), without the mitigation of a brine, will lose so much juice that, it

seems to me, one should simply never go there. Less juice means not only less juiciness, but less flavour.

As mentioned earlier, juice will start forming in the steak as soon as the intracellular (cell-wall, phospholipid) fat starts to melt in earnest. It will accumulate and remain in the steak at an optimal volume just before the muscle fibres have separated enough to release it completely.

Another very important factor in preserving the heavenly juices in your steak is resting time. Most steaks will constrict as they cook. More than just shrinking from moisture loss, the muscle fibres tighten under the assault of heat, increasing the internal turgidity of the meat. Cutting into your steak at this point will release meat juices at pressure, leaving much less inside the steak where you want it. The appropriate length of resting time depends on the strength of the muscle, as well as the size of the steak. Thick sirloin, tri-tip, and bavette—all part of muscle groups that do a fair amount of work in the live animal—need ample resting time. Striploin and rib eye need less resting time, pound for pound. The goal is to allow enough time for your steak to relax after cooking, effectively depressurizing it, allowing its juices to take up residence in the greater space afforded to them. Sometimes this takes 10 minutes, sometimes longer.

A steak, especially a large one, should rest on aluminum foil, and be very loosely wrapped in order to

TASTES LIKE CHICKEN?

You may hear that fats in meat give it flavour. That's true, but maybe not in the way you think. The fat you can see does indeed lend a nice texture and moisture to meats, but it's the fat you can't see that allows us to distinguish the taste of different species. An animal's diet can certainly change the taste of visible fat and meat, but all things being equal, the different tastes of lamb, chicken, beef, and pork are signalled by the fat that makes up the cell walls of these animals. This invisible fat is a phospholipid, is unsaturated, and has a rather different omega-6 to omega-3 profile. Without it, all meats would taste virtually the same.

gather the juices that flow out. It's important to keep the foil loose enough to allow the steak to cool, as the inertia from cooking will propel the temperature of the steak higher even after it's removed from the heat.

Tear off a sheet of foil larger than you would need to wrap the steak. Lay the sheet down on a flat surface and place the steak on top. Loosely gather up the foil around the steak so heat can escape while the juices are captured in the foil. Some juice will actually be reabsorbed into the meat, but some won't. You can serve any juices poured overtop of the steak, or in a soy dish or ramekin, which is fun and just seems more thoughtful.

THE TAKEAWAY FOR SUPREME JUICINESS:
Get your steak off the heat as it approaches medium-rare (at 120°F to 125°F), not after. Let it rest wrapped very loosely in foil for 10 minutes, depending on the size and to some extent the tenderness of your steak. When the steak relaxes, it's ready for your knife. Don't worry about the steak not being piping hot. Good steak is best enjoyed just a bit warmer than the temperature of your tongue.

THAT'S JUICE, NOT BLOOD

The red juices from steak are just that: juices (not blood). Blood would congeal when exposed to air, which is why it is used to make things like boudin (blood sausage). Steak juice (the "jus") is actually intracellular fluid containing myoglobin, a protein similar to hemoglobin that uses iron to fix oxygen close to muscle tissues that need it quickly for hard work in the live animal. Myoglobin turns red when it is first exposed to oxygen. Red meat belongs mostly to larger, hard-working beasts, and white meat to smaller ones that don't have as many demands on their muscles, since moving around is less taxing. Cows and all other mammals (and some fish) contain varying levels of myoglobin in different muscles. Think chicken thigh versus chicken breast. The goal when cooking steak is to keep as much of these delicious juices inside the steak as possible, instead of losing them to the grill, the pan, or your plate.

SALTWATER BRINE

It may seem odd to brine steaks, but there are times when it can do wonders, especially for larger, leaner cuts. When salt penetrates the meat, it denatures the protein, breaking the hydrogen bonds that give it a particular shape. Denatured proteins coil up, allowing them to hold more water—up to 15% more—and some of that extra water is not as readily evicted from the meat during cooking. The result is a moister, saltier (in a good way) steak that interacts marvellously well with the smoky flavours of wood or charcoal. Although not the main reason to brine, brined raw meat will also keep a couple of days longer in the fridge. Here is a simple brine recipe for steaks:

8 CUPS COLD WATER
1/2 CUP SALT
1/4 CUP PACKED BROWN SUGAR

IN A BOWL, combine water, salt, and brown sugar, and stir until the sugar and salt have dissolved. (Alternatively, you can also brine your steak in a resealable bag.) Submerge your steak in the brine (double or triple this mixture if needed). Cover and refrigerate for 3 to 6 hours, depending on the size of your steak. A 1-inch-thick sirloin slice needs about 4 hours. A 2-inch-thick (or more) sirloin slice needs a full 6 hours. When you're ready, remove steak from the brine and pat it dry with paper towels or a tea towel. It's now ready to cook the way you like it. It will behave a little differently, so check for doneness carefully. If you like your steaks above medium-rare (125°F), brining first may be the way to go.

GREAT MOMENTS IN STEAK

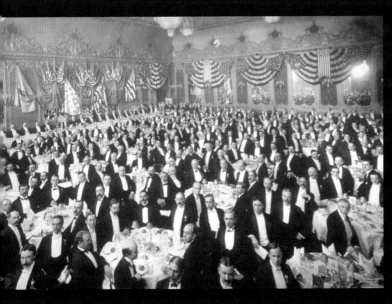

The Sons of the Revolution in the State of New York at their steak banquet at Delmonico's, New York City, 1906.

Notice anything peculiar about this photo? The distinct lack of diversity was typical of the times, spanning from the end of the U.S. Civil War to the end of the 19th century. Steak banquets—the steak- and beer-fuelled precursors to the steakhouse—were the domain of white males of the moneyed class. They talked politics and raised money for their ventures, guzzling beer and devouring huge quantities of beef, a tradition borrowed from the English, who by then had been doing this for nearly two centuries.

Steakhouse restaurants only began to proliferate after the invention of the refrigerated railcar. Before that, cattle drivers drove cattle to rail hubs in the American Midwest, then the cows were loaded live onto cars. By the time they reached the lucrative markets in New York, Chicago, and Philadelphia, the cows that hadn't died from the stress of these journeys had lost so much weight that it made the price of beefsteak prohibitive to everyone except the elite.

After many failed attempts, refrigerated cars became more common. By the late 1870s, railcars loaded with blocks of ice made shipping beef (as opposed to live animals) possible, if still somewhat risky and certainly labour intensive. It would be almost another 100 years before these moving iceboxes would be completely replaced by mechanically powered refrigerated railcars. The last ice-loaded railcars were all but gone by 1960.

Some of the old steakhouses that grew out of the success of the refrigerated railcar are still very much around, serving up steak dinners to hungry patrons: Delmonico's, credited by some to have first served the rib eye (which is why it is sometimes called a Delmonico steak), opened in 1837 and has survived to this day in several iterations and locations. Peter Luger Steak House, also in New York, has been grilling steaks since 1887; The Palm has been operating since 1926; Gene and Georgetti in Chicago opened its doors in 1941; and Hy's hung its shingle above a women's clothing store in Calgary in 1955.

SALT

SALT has been integral to cooking for thousands of years, enabled societies throughout history to preserve and transport food, and, in general, contributed significantly to human civilization. But salt, like fat, has been unfairly categorized as bad for our health, even though we need some salt in our diet to maintain critical physiological functions and to regulate fluid levels in our bodies. In fact, if we become salt deficient, we can develop very serious problems very quickly.

Interestingly, recommended dietary intake levels of salt no longer enjoy the consensus they once did. (See "It's Time to End the War on Salt" by Melinda Wenner Moyer in the July 8, 2011, issue of *Scientific American*, for instance.) Current guidelines call for no more than 1 teaspoon of sodium per day, but the lead researcher on a major worldwide study published in *The Lancet* in July 2016 suggested that acceptable levels could actually be at least twice that amount.

Salt has an enormous effect not only on the taste of beef, but on how it behaves as it cooks. I recommend using Celtic-style sea salt or a true rock salt (like natural Himalayan salt or natural rock salt) because they contain other water-active minerals that raise pH enough to create a slightly basic (less acidic) surface on steak, which I find helps the browning process, resulting in a more delicious crust. I also find these salts are just tastier in general. When it comes to culinary uses, it's true that not all salt is created equal.

The natural salt in foods like beets, peanuts, fish, and meat makes up a significant part of their taste profile, and they taste good to us because we have evolved to like a certain amount of saltiness. By salting food we are, in effect, tricking our taste buds into thinking we are eating something different—perhaps something on the whole more nutritious—than we actually are. Balance is the key: not too much, and not too little. Your tongue knows, and that is why cookbooks so often tell you to "salt to taste."

Dusting your steak with a fair amount of salt, sometimes called "dry brining," also helps it hang on to a little more moisture while it cooks. At first the salt will draw water out of the meat, but if left alone, that moisture will be reabsorbed, pulling briny flavour deep into the steak and, to a certain extent, denaturing the meat protein (which allows it to hold on to more moisture). The trick is in giving the salt a little time to do its work before cooking. Salt your meat liberally, then wait at least 30 minutes. Generally speaking, the longer you wait the better—up to a day or two, keeping your seasoned steak in the fridge until you need it.

People sometimes freak out a little when they see how much salt I use when I'm preparing a steak for the grill, but none of those people have failed to be impressed by the final result. There is a saying in Argentine asado cooking—one of my absolute favourite steak traditions—that translates as "trust the salt." It means that you don't need to flavour steak with anything else, and that the right amount of salt will take care of a lot. The Argentines even have a specially graded salt for grilling meat, steaks in particular, called *sal parrillera*. Not too coarse, not too fine, it's just right for distributing evenly over steak.

HOW MUCH SALT SHOULD YOU USE? 1/2 teaspoon of salt sprinkled over 2 pounds of meat will do the trick.

THE THREE BEST WAYS TO COOK STEAK
GRILL, FRY, REVERSE-SEAR

Now that you know what to look for when choosing a perfectly delicious steak, let's consider the three best ways to cook it: grilling, frying, and reverse-searing. You can push any steak to perform reasonably well using any one of these methods, but you will have much more satisfying results when you can properly connect the right steak to the right method.

GRILLING

The biggest advantage to grilling a steak over charcoal or gas flame is that you can create an environment that is both hot and dry. Using a gas grill, the cooking environment is somewhat less dry, since the combustion of propane or natural gas produces some water vapour. (If you doubt this, hold a glass a few inches above your gas flame for a second and watch it fog up.) Hardwood lump charcoal (which is my favourite way to grill steak) burns significantly hotter than gas. Still, gas offers a more than tolerable alternative to charcoal grilling.

This hot, dry way of cooking works well for thicker steaks because you can develop a flavourful crust without the impediment of moisture, and add flavour to the steak as it connects with smoky and gaseous flavour compounds. Grilling also helps to avoid poaching, since the moisture outside of the steak evaporates quickly, letting the meat inside the steak cook by conduction from adjacent mass instead of from steam. It also works well for marinated steaks, which will have taken on moisture, some of which they will readily expel (if cooked in a pan this would lead to serious disappointment). Drippings from marinated steaks on gas grills and charcoal simply add to the smoky flavour effects.

The development of a nice dark crust is key to being able to manage your steak properly on the grill. As the steak darkens, its surface will harden, and the previously sticky proteins will bond with sugars, causing it to lose its grip on the grill. This allows you to turn the steak without leaving some of it attached to the grating. Achieving a good crust is also one of the factors that, along with relative weight, shrink, firmness, and bounce (from pressing with one's finger) lets experienced steak cooks know when the steak has achieved optimal doneness.

Steaks that are between 3/4 inch and 2 inches thick are ideal for grilling. For really, really thick steaks (over 2 inches thick), unless you are prepared to manage your

grill for a longer cooking session, hotter grilling can be a challenge. Your steak may end up charred, with a worn-out, frayed crust, or unevenly cooked, or dry due to heat stress compressing the meat and expelling its juices. There are, of course, remedies. In fact, some steak cuisines not only account for long grilling times with gigantic steaks, but seek them out. These steak masters, like the asadors of Argentina, create slower cooking temperatures by burning down wood or charcoal to cooler embers, or by raising the meat farther above a hotter fire. Accomplished backyard grillers will develop a crust on the hot part of their grills, then adjust the coal or gas to create cooler parts, and then cover the grill to roast the steak. This also creates an opportunity to add incredible smoky flavours by adding a little wood to the charcoal (or right on top of the heating plate in gas grills; see page 49 for more).

For most thinner steaks (less than 3/4 inch thick), a hot grill will simply cook the meat too quickly. You won't get a crust at all, and you run the risk of over-cooking your steak. If you let the coals cool or turn the gas down, you won't be able to generate enough heat, which leaves too much moisture on the surface of the meat, impeding browning and encouraging poaching. A poached steak has just one possible texture, and it's never what you want.

THE TAKEAWAY FOR GRILLING STEAK:
Grilling adds divine smoky flavour and colour in a hot, dry environment, and is ideal for any steak between 1 and 2 inches thick. (With the exception of skirts and flanks, truly thin steaks don't do as well on a grill.) Poaching is easily avoided here, so you can cook moist, marinated steaks perfectly.

FRYING

As long as your cooking surface is hot enough, frying can be just the right way to cook a steak. A sufficiently hot pan will overcome the moisture on the surface of your steak and help it develop a tasty crust. By "hot" I mean hot enough so that when you hold your hand above the surface of your pan or griddle, you know immediately that it would be a terrible idea to actually touch the pan. To achieve this temperature, preheat your dry pan for about 5 minutes over high heat on an average household stovetop. I recommend using a heavy cast-iron pan, heavy-grade stainless-steel pan, or a frying pan that has a "cookie" bottom, all of which absorb, hold, and conduct heat more evenly.

Frying really should be done with the aid of some kind of fat, to prevent sticking and to help cook the steak more evenly (the fat helps distribute the heat over the surface of the meat). Since I know you're not a vegetarian, this might as well be animal fat (lard, tallow, duck fat, bacon fat, chicken fat, or a combination of butter and another oil to raise the butter's smoking point). Animal fats—with the exception of butter, which contains milk solids—have a higher smoking point and are generally more stable at higher temperatures. They also have the advantage of being saturated and unprocessed. Vegetable oils meant for cooking are highly processed to raise their smoking points. They are also unsaturated fats, meaning that they can create toxic free radicals in your food, especially at high cooking temperatures, so it's best to avoid them.

Even though you can heat a pan to temperatures in excess of 400°F on a stovetop, the temperature will plummet the moment the surface of the pan comes into contact with your steak. But we can work with this. Some decrease in temperature is actually desirable, since we are cooking with a thin to moderately thick steak (between very thin to less than 1 inch thick), and that steak will cook internally quite quickly.

Frying is just as active an activity as grilling, perhaps more so. You must watch and tend to your steak in the pan, taking advantage of the whole surface for its searing, crust-making hot spots, as well as its cooler, mellower spots. If your pan is not hot enough, your steak will cool the pan to the point where it is just hot enough to drain the steak of its juices, which will bubble up and steam your steak, poaching it to an unrecoverable greyness and woolly interior.

For steaks with fulsome fat caps, you can melt the cap to cook the steak in its own fat. Using tongs, simply hold the steak cap-side down on the hot pan until enough liquid fat renders and pools in the bottom of the pan.

Whichever fat you use for frying, your goal is to sear your steak and quickly develop a crust, while cooking it to just under medium-rare (about 120°F) or a little higher for medium-rare. Pan-frying also creates the opportunity to baste your steak (see page 65) and to make pan sauces when your steak is happily resting (which it should do for at least a full 5 minutes or a little longer; see pages 25–26).

THE TAKEAWAY FOR FRYING STEAK: If your pan is hot enough, frying creates a nice crust quickly, without overcooking the steak. This method works best for thin and moderately thick steaks (just under 1 inch thick). For a 1/4-inch striploin, frying is quite possibly the surest way to steak bliss. Some fat in the pan is necessary, preferably animal fat. Frying is a gateway to basting recipes and delicious pan sauces.

REVERSE-SEARING

Reverse-searing is a tremendously useful technique for cooking larger, thicker steaks. It provides a great deal of control over doneness and leads to a perfect crust, right at the end when the steak is seared. This method is great for steaks between 1 and 3 inches in thickness (or more, if you're that sort of person, but then we're really talking about a roast beef, aren't we?).

Reverse-seared steaks are first slowly cooked to near-doneness in a low-temperature oven, then seared very quickly in a hot pan on the stovetop. The only extra things you really need are an abundance of time and an instant-read thermometer.

Slow heat cooks the meat evenly all the way through, allowing a gradual breakdown of tissue, enzymatic action at low heat (which makes the steak more tender), and the melting of fat. It will also dry out the surface of the steak so that when it comes time for the final sear in the pan, a delectable crust will form almost instantly with much less smoke than it would take to sear it before oven cooking. (So, if you live in an apartment, or can't open the windows in your house because it's freezing cold out, you have another reason to be thankful for this method of cooking.)

When reverse-searing, it's important to note that you aren't fully cooking the steak in the oven. You are *almost* cooking it through. You finish cooking by searing the steak in the pan for just a couple of minutes, raising the temperature of your steak another 5°F or more. You move your steak from the oven to the stovetop when

IF YOU WANT TO SEAR AND THEN OVEN COOK

If you're short on time, have a thick steak on hand (1 1/2 inches or more), and need to cook indoors, follow this short-cut method. Preheat your oven to 400°F. Meanwhile, heat a dry pan on your stovetop until it is truly hot—a full 5 minutes over high heat. Anoint one side of your steak with the fat or oil of your choice—just enough to coat—then place steak fat-side down in the pan. Leave the steak alone for about 3 to 4 minutes, until you can see the edges bordering the underside of the steak darken, indicating that the surface on the pan side has in fact darkened nicely. (The searing will probably throw off a lot of smoke, so make sure your exhaust fan is on.) Turn the steak over, turn off the stovetop, and immediately transfer the pan to the preheated oven. Roast the steak, uncovered, for 12 minutes per pound of meat. (Use less time for cuts that are thinner, even if they are just as heavy.)

your steak reads an average of 118°F, or 115°F in the thickest, meatiest part of the middle. Depending on the size and shape of your steak, oven cooking takes about 30 minutes per pound of meat (for steaks 1 1/2 pounds or more) to get the steak to its desired pre-sear temperature. Steaks that are fairly heavy but spread out and not that thick will be brought up to temperature more quickly than a thicker steak of the same weight.

When oven cooking first, the slow increase in the steak's temperature also means that the meat is far less stressed from the heat, allowing some structures to break down without pressurizing the meat, which might otherwise squeeze out its juices. The meat loses less moisture overall than it does using the sear-then-oven method, and it cooks much more evenly. I'm so fond of the reverse-sear that I'm only going to advise using the sear-then-oven method in this one instance: Do it only if you don't have time to reverse-sear. (If you feel you need to sear your steak and then oven cook it, take a look at the sidebar above.)

When reverse-searing, your oven will be occupied for a relatively long time, and at a low temperature (anywhere from 180°F to 225°F), so be prepared to make the rest of the meal using the stovetop. (On the bright side, you will have time to cook everything else at an even pace, perhaps with a glass of something to improve your patience and, if necessary, your humour.) Marginal improvements to texture and tenderness can be made by bringing the steak up to its pre-sear temperature in a lower-temperature oven (like 180°F, and I wouldn't try anything lower than that), but 225°F works perfectly well. This is the temperature I use in the recipes in this book, since it gives more than adequate results in less time. You may lose a smidgen more moisture at this higher temperature, but the difference is not that noticeable. You can cook the steak directly on the middle rack of your oven, lining the rack below with a sheet of aluminum foil to catch any moisture that drops out of the steak, which will prevent your oven from smoking the next time you use it. I use a wire cooling rack to support the steak in the oven, which allows hot, dry air to circulate freely around the meat, drying out the surface. Turn the steak once, halfway through its pre-searing time, to ensure the surface dries evenly.

When it comes time to sear your steak (when the steak reaches an internal temperature of 115°F in the meaty middle, or an average of 118°F when tested in different parts of the steak), have a very hot pan at the ready. Coat one side of your steak with a little fat or oil of your choice, or hold the fat cap to the hot pan until enough fat renders out, then sear both sides for about 1 minute each, or until you like the crust and the steak has an internal temperature approaching 125°F in the meaty middle. Remove it from the pan and let rest for about 4 minutes, uncovered (longer won't hurt).

THE TAKEAWAY FOR REVERSE-SEARING STEAK: Slowly cook steaks that are more than 1 inch thick and up to 2 1/2 inches or more in a 180°F to 225°F oven, then sear them with a little fat in a very hot pan. The pre-sear takes 30 minutes per pound of meat for steaks weighing 1 1/2 pounds or more. Remove steak from the oven when it reaches an average temperature of 118°F, or 115°F in the meaty middle. Use an instant-read thermometer to take the steak's temperature for the pre-sear, and the sear itself. Stop searing when you have nice crust and the internal temperature of the steak is approaching 125°F in the meaty middle. This method provides lots of control for perfect doneness and enhanced texture and tenderness, with less resting time and searing time (though more cooking time).

WHY MEDIUM-RARE MATTERS

There comes a point during the cooking of steak when everything comes into perfect, delectable alignment. The juices have loosened but are stable, the fat is just the right sort of melty, the meat's fibres have become defined but not overly so, and the meat is supple while the crust is dark and full of complex, savoury flavour. If this point of alignment has a temperature, I would name it 125°F (in the centre of the steak), or even a little lower. The French, appropriately, call this simply *à point*, which translates to something a bit under medium-rare in North America.

The North American standard of medium-rare is generally in the 130°F to 135°F range. The reasons why I recommend cooking a steak to a few degrees below that are threefold:

1. Your steak will simply lose too much juice when cooked to above 130°F.
2. Your steak will continue cooking a few degrees higher after you remove it from the heat, even without tenting or wrapping.
3. An opportunity to taste the full potential of steak is lost when there is no rare steak left in the bite, and that seems a shame. When a bite of steak has a mostly even but still varied level of doneness, its full potential is realized.

I find that most medium-rare steak eaters actually do like a certain, if small amount, of rare steak in the very middle. Generally speaking, when any given whole steak is cooked to 120°F, much of it will also reach medium-rare or even medium, 5 to 10 degrees hotter. Indeed, an important part of eating a rather well-aged rib steak or porterhouse is experiencing the varied textures in a single piece of meat: some mostly uncooked meat amid well-done, crusted meat in the vicinity of medium-rare meat, where the juices are liberated in a mouthful. It's a nearly unfathomably pleasurable experience.

A single steak can contain several different types of tissues. For example, a slice of sirloin consists of three or more muscles, which cook at different rates and which behave differently at different levels of doneness. Rib steak has three adjacent muscles. Porterhouse consists of two distinctly different muscles separated by bone. Cooking all of these steaks to an average temperature of 120°F takes care of these variations. Some parts of the steak will be more red and softer, others will be darker and coarser, and other parts—most parts—will be what a typical enthusiastic steak eater (in my experience) knows to be medium-rare. Yes, some rareness will endure closer to the bone or inside denser tissue, but isn't that better than a medium-well done steak?

After a steak has been removed from the heat, a certain amount of thermal inertia continues to propel its temperature upward. The hotter and longer the steak was cooking, the more inertia there is, and the longer it will take for the temperature to level out and then cool. That's why the slow, reverse-searing method requires less resting time and why a steak pulled from the fire as it approaches 125°F is going to finish close to 130°F in any case, before it begins to cool.

STAGES OF PERFECTION

Steak doneness ("colour" to a grill cook) can be a sensitive business. For the purposes of this book, and I think in the world at large, this guide should give you all you need to hit the colour you are looking for, whether cooking at home or directing your server in a restaurant.

1. BLUE

The steak is very much raw, and just a little warm to the touch. If the whole steak is cooked this way, it is only seared or very quickly charred. The middles of rare, *à point*, and medium-rare steaks are very often on the raw side, too. There is very little juice in a steak that is blue all the way through, though; the juice is still well contained within the structure of the steak and none of the fat has melted. Not many steaks are that good blue, but there are exceptions, given your mood. I've had terrific well-aged steak quickly seared and served to me barely warm—a sublimely dark and richly concentrated filet mignon

springs to memory. I still secretly wished it had been cooked 2 minutes longer.

INTERNAL TEMPERATURE: 85°F TO 100°F

2. RARE

The steak is well cooked close to the surface, with fibres beginning to loosen partway through, and much of its interior is still raw, but warm. Some crust, and some juice, since the cooked part of the structure of the steak has been disrupted. Very good aged steaks can be excellent rare.

INTERNAL TEMPERATURE BEFORE RESTING: 100°F TO 115°F

3. À POINT

This is, as you might have imagined, how the French might order their steak and how I prefer it most of the time: "on the point of" … perfection, in my view. It takes full advantage of the silky texture of steak with a substantial but not dominating, partially raw, warm middle, loosening the fibres just enough to free the juices and melt the fat while giving it enough time to develop a tasty crust. I nearly always try to cook steaks for myself to this level of doneness, and order steak "rare to medium-rare" in restaurants.

INTERNAL TEMPERATURE BEFORE RESTING: 115°F TO 120°F

The photo opposite shows pieces from the same cut of steak (from the prime rib). Notice how the slices get smaller as they are more cooked. This is because the steak loses its juices (water and fat) the longer it is on the heat. The exact temperatures of the steak slices in the photo, from bottom to top, before resting: 92°F, 104°F, 119°F, 126°F, 135°F.

1.

2.

3.

4.

5.

4. MEDIUM-RARE

My second favourite "colour" of doneness, medium-rare is really the slightly more done, go-to equivalent of *à point* everywhere in the world outside of France. There can be a noticeable bit of warm, partially raw meat in the middle, but otherwise the fibres are well loosened, releasing their juices but still holding some. Much of the time the steak will just start to feel grainy near the surface and partway through, but a great medium-rare steak can be evenly cooked and juicy throughout.

INTERNAL TEMPERATURE BEFORE RESTING:
120°F TO 130°F

5. MEDIUM

Some steaks get to medium and perform pretty well. They are almost always quite fatty and engorged (like prime rib). For my money, though, this is the absolute end of the story, since anything after this point is simply overdone. If you like meat that way, I think you would do much better with a slow roast, braised meat, or low-and-slow barbecue, which, as so many of us already know, can be supernaturally tasty. The texture of medium grilled or pan-fried meat can be pretty grainy, especially for lean cuts. A little medium meat is part of what happens to big steaks on the grill at their extremities, and that's okay, since they are generally tempered by an extra-juicy environment and in the vicinity of rarer meat. If the whole steak is cooked to medium, the juice has mostly left the steak and is on the plate, or lost altogether to the coals.

INTERNAL TEMPERATURE BEFORE RESTING:
130°F TO 135°F

SLICING AND SERVING

CARVE YOUR WAY TO TENDERNESS AND PERFECT PRESENTATION

BETTER SLICING MEANS LESS CHEWING

I've never been one to shy away from a little chew. In fact, sometimes it's simply part of the experience of any given cut. Coarser meat can be very tasty and satisfying indeed, and as long as it is not a task to chew it, no one is going to complain that the divine morsel on their fork doesn't fall apart like a bit of birthday cake on their tongue.

That said, it is important to max out the tenderness any time you can with every steak you serve, unless the steak is already so soft that it doesn't matter. For the less tender cuts—hanger steak, some sirloin, flank, bavette, culotte, and other cuts farther away from the centre of the beast—slicing can make the difference between a perfectly cooked steak that is a bit of a bore to chew, and one that is just a really satisfying bite. In these cases, the direction and length of the grain becomes really important.

You can determine the grain direction by looking for fibres or parallel "stripes" in the meat. It's more visible in some cuts than others. When in doubt, consult the first page of each chapter in Part Two, which gives an overview of each cut.

The grain in a steak generally runs one of three ways: widthwise, lengthwise, or from top to bottom (that is, from the top surface of the steak to its underside; the steak's "height," as it were). Sometimes, however, the grain will change direction. Steaks with top-to-bottom grain will already have short fibres, which means you can't go far wrong when slicing. But by cutting steaks with widthwise or lengthwise grain across those longer fibres, you can increase the tenderness of these tasty cuts immensely.

I've seen analogies to wood cutting, and they work pretty well. Like wood, muscle derives tensile strength along its length. A stick of cedar kindling is much harder to cut across its width than it is to split through its length, because cutting is actually severing fibres, and splitting is merely separating them.

If we had teeth like knives, we might never have to worry about our steak-slicing strategy. But our teeth, especially our molars, where most chewing takes place, are more like grinders and separators, so fibres are much easier to pull apart than cut through. Some steaks, like flank, have grain that runs down the length of its shape, which means that the natural way of slicing it is already across its grain, significantly shortening

the fibres so you can pull them apart instead of biting through, and chewiness won't be an issue. For other steaks, like bavette, which in its natural, unsliced state is actually more tender than a flank steak, the grain runs across its width. One might be tempted to slice the bavette parallel to the grain, but that could land you with a much less tender steak than you had anticipated—less tender than its flank cousin, for instance.

Finally, some steaks, like most of a rib steak and all of a striploin, have fibres that run through the steak from top to bottom. In both of these cuts, it simply doesn't matter which way you slice them because these steaks are naturally tender. With a sirloin, though, it might, because it's not as tender to begin with. Since there is no obvious way to cut a steak with top-to-bottom fibres across the grain, your best approach is to slice the less tender cuts on a bias—that is, with your (very sharp) knife tilted at a manageable angle away from you as you slice through the steak.

Cutting on a bias will shorten the fibres, too, because you are effectively cutting each fibre at a different point along its length. This means your slice will be a shorter, more tender, cross-section. The key here is not to cut your steak too thinly. If your slices are really thin, the juices have nowhere to go but onto your carving board. The exception is for cold cooked steak. (There are next-day steak recipes in this book that call for thin slices, such as the Steak Canapés on page 158 and the Ultimate Steak Sandwich on page 163.) Once a cooked steak has been refrigerated, the fats will have mostly resolidified and reintegrated into the meat, so you can cut it as thinly as you need to. For a freshly cooked steak, though, it's generally best to cut across the grain in 1/2-inch slices, shortening the grain while keeping juices inside the meat.

A side benefit to cutting a steak before serving it is that you can see how well you've cooked it, giving you a second shot at bringing it up to temperature if you need to, or putting an overdone steak aside for another use if it's too far gone. In my view, big, whole, crowd-sating steaks are at their dressiest best sliced and fanned out on a board or platter. Individually portioned steaks look great on the plate cut into beefy 1/2-inch slices (or thicker, depending on the size, shape, and post-cut tenderness of your steak).

Tenderness in general is far more complicated than it seems. The truth is that not everyone agrees which steaks are inherently tender and which ones are not. Industry professionals use a gauge with sensors called the Warner-Bratzler shear (WBS) to measure tenderness in muscle groups. We humans, however, perceive other things. For example, the amount of fat in a particular cut lubricates the meat, making it feel looser and suppler on our tongues and cheeks—that is, more tender. The consistency of muscle fibres, even when short and fine, can make some cuts feel grainy or drier—on the whole, less tender. To me, these different aspects of steak just make it all the more magical, leading to an overall sense that what we're eating is simply fantastic, with comparative tenderness all but forgotten.

We can all agree that the tenderloin (in a cow, the psoas major muscle) is truly tender, case closed. But is it really better than a sirloin (serratus ventralis, among other muscles), with its different textures, melty fat, and satisfying heft? The serratus ventralis, the most tender of all sirloin muscles, ranks as tougher on the WBS scale than the tenderloin (7.81 to 6.85, if it matters), but I would rather grill up a beefy sirloin than a filet anytime.

HOW TO SLICE STEAKS WITH WIDTH-WISE GRAIN

Steaks with grain that runs across their width include many of my favourites, such as bavette, hanger, and skirt. The photos and text that follow provide some tips to help you maximize the tenderness of these flavourful cuts.

SHORTER GRAIN HOLDS LESS JUICE

Steaks with shorter grain running vertically through the meat may be naturally tender, but they wick out juices more easily than steaks with grain running across the length or width, so you should take extra care when checking for doneness. Check early, and remove them from the heat a little earlier if you have to.

LESS TENDER: This bavette is cut *with* the grain (along the fibres instead of across them). The steak will be less tender, even if it holds a little more juice, because you have to sever the fibres with your teeth.

MORE TENDER: This bavette is sliced across the grain, severing and shortening the fibres to just the width of the slice. That makes the steak easy to chew, because you don't have to break through the fibres but merely pull them apart.

LESS TENDER: This hanger steak is sliced along its grain. The fibres remain long and are therefore tougher to chew. The steak will be less tender even if it holds a little more juice, becasue you have to sever the fibres with your teeth.

MORE TENDER: This hanger steak is sliced across its grain. The fibres are in shorter cross-sections, which makes them easier to chew. You can either slice the steak diagonally across its length, as shown here, or cut the steak in half first (across its width), then rotate it 90 degrees, and slice it across the grain (in which case, your slices will be longer).

From left to right: 5 1/2-inch boning knife, 10-inch butcher's knife, 8-inch chef's knife, 8-inch honing steel.

KEEP IT SHARP

IT REALLY IS IMPORTANT TO OWN AND MAINTAIN A HIGH-QUALITY, SHARP KNIFE FOR CARVING.

The most versatile is the all-purpose chef's knife. Chef's knives (sometimes called cook's knives) are generally 8 inches in length, with a thick, wide blade that curves from the hilt to a pointed tip, allowing for a rocking motion when needed.

The standard butcher's knife, usually 8 to 10 inches long with a wide blade (but not as thick as the chef's knife), is another great tool. The blade curves abruptly close to the tip, which helps for cutting evenly through broad steaks.

The boning knife, with its shorter, narrow blade and extreme point, is very handy for deboning and carving around bones.

In either case, keeping your carving knives sharp is essential. A dull knife is more likely to slip over the surface of food rather than cut into it. And because you're likely applying more pressure to achieve the result you want, the chances of your dull knife slipping are pretty high, making using one a dangerous proposition. Dull knives also make a mess of your steak, because the dull force will crush the meat instead of cutting through it, sending juices everywhere and making deliberate, tidy slices nearly impossible.

To maintain a proper edge on your knife you need to "hone" it between sharpenings using a honing steel. In the course of normal use, the blade of a chef's knife (or any sharp knife that isn't serrated) will actually start to fold over itself—structurally, the molecules of steel become misaligned, pointed in various directions instead of facing the same way. This results in a dull edge. To straighten things out, you need to pass a honing steel along the edge of the blade. As long as the edge hasn't dulled past the point of no return, which it eventually will and in which case you then need to actually sharpen it, honing will correct your blade without shaving off any material.

To be clear, honing a knife does not sharpen it. It simply re-straightens the knife edge. Sharpening abrasively removes some metal from the knife to re-establish its edge. Sharpening can be done much less frequently than honing.

HOW AND WHEN TO HONE YOUR KNIFE

If you are new to honing, I recommend that you hold the handle of the honing steel comfortably in front of you, with the tip of the steel pointing at a downward angle facing away from you. With your other hand, starting with the heel (widest part) of the blade, draw the blade at a 15-degree angle across the steel, so the point of contact slides from the heel to the tip of the blade in one complete motion, away from you. Repeat with the other side of the blade on the other side of the steel, alternating sides about 20 times. Do this every time you feel your knife beginning to lose its razor-sharp edge. I generally hone my knife before every use.

Experienced honers will hold the honing steel upright in front of them, stroking the knife across the blade toward the handle, relying on experience (and the cross-guard, which is the widened part of the handle where it meets the steel shaft) to keep the edge away from their hand.

HOW AND WHEN TO SHARPEN YOUR KNIFE

Sharpening shouldn't happen nearly as often as honing. This is good, because it's more work. I rather enjoy it, though, the same way motorheads enjoy polishing up their ride. Taking care of your knives will help you to develop a healthy respect for them. Even when they're not sharpened, they are sharp!

Before getting into sharpening techniques, there are some rules you should follow to keep safe (believe me, I have learned them from experience):

1. Never show off—to yourself or anyone— while cutting anything. I did that … once.
2. When you have finished cutting, clean your knife and put it away. A magnetic knife rack or knife block is preferable for storage, but a drawer will do. Untended knives end up getting covered by something, or turned around, or knocked on the floor when you are preparing something else, and are a hazard.
3. Always make sure your hands are dry when you are handling a knife; otherwise, it can easily slip.
4. You rarely need to apply a lot of force to cut something with a knife. If you think you do, try another approach.
5. Stay focused. If there is a baby crying for your attention behind you, or a pot boiling over, stop cutting.
6. Avoid using knives for things other than cutting. Sure, there are exceptions. Opening cans isn't one of them.

When the time comes to actually sharpen your knife, the easiest and cheapest way to do it yourself is with a combination grit stone. It's about the size of a stick of butter, with a coarse side and a finer side. Soak it in water for 5 minutes, then put the stone on a kitchen towel on a flat surface, so that it doesn't slide. In a single motion, gently and evenly stroke the blade, edge side toward you, diagonally across the stone. The blade edge should contact the stone at a 15- to 20-degree angle, with the dull side about 1/8 inch higher than the blade edge. You don't have to apply much pressure—if your stone moves, you're pressing too hard. Repeat on each side about 20 times, and then hone the blade on a steel. Sharpen your blade every month or two, depending on how much you use your knife, or take it to a professional sharpener.

For more on knife safety, knife handling, and knife skills in general, I recommend taking a short workshop or day course. I took a course from Peter Hertzmann, author of the rather useful book *Knife Skills Illustrated* (W. W. Norton & Company, 2007).

THE INS AND OUTS OF COOKING

ON WOOD, CHARCOAL, AND GAS GRILLS

Making fire is as primal as we can get. When paired with steak, things get pretty interesting. Our ancient ancestors managed to hunt many species of large mammal to extinction over the last 15,000 years. The 50 million years leading up to that point, before we had the numbers or inclination to meaningfully interfere in their demise, was the Cenozoic era, often referred to as the Age of Mammals. They lived on every continent except Antarctica, with herds so enormous they covered the vista to the horizon, like a continent-sized ant-covered jar of jam. They survived huge fluctuations in climate and environment, and managed to see their way to the other side of 20 Ice Ages, until the most recent one, the one where we happened.

Most animals heavier than 400 pounds—giant camels, gargantuan ground sloths, woolly rhinoceros, mastodons, woolly mammoths, giant armadillos, and so many more, including the gigantic aurochs—the cow's direct ancestor—were forever ripped from the prairie and forest, never to be seen again, between 200 and 2,000 years of *Homo erectus* arriving.

We used their bones as tools, as weapons, as building blocks, and as fuel for fire, and their hides as shelter and clothing. And of course we used their meat, ringing in the first real population spike in our often brutal history, outpaced only by the advent of widespread agriculture centuries later. Within this frenzied era of hunting, we also learned how to control fire, and with that came cooking.

It is only in this long retrospect, a perspective not possible for early humans, that we can understand our impact on the world we once shared with these large beasts. What remains of those ancient days, when we cook on fire now, is an innate and powerful sense, regardless of our cultural origins, that the activity is not a new one. From the very first cookout I can remember as a young boy, something old inside me was roused by the smoke and crackle of the cooking fire, and the way it changed the hitherto uninteresting meat placed upon it into the deeply flavoured nourishment I came to know as dinner.

When I get the opportunity to cook on actual wood with a live fire, I usually jump at the chance, burning logs to embers, and adding slow-burning wood to the embers to achieve a graded fire with consistent, deliberate levels of heat. The result is a smokier steak (delightfully so) and a smokier cook (also delightful, though my wife does not always agree). Most often, though, I'm cooking over hardwood charcoal (in my view, the second-best way to cook steak), followed by the gas grill. The gas grill certainly has its advantages and convenience, enduring heat being key among them. Gas comes in second for a few reasons, low peak temperature being the main one.

I have an old Weber 20-inch kettle barbecue that my brother found at the back of his country lot one day. I set it in my back yard among rocks I pilfered from the side of some highway construction years ago. The kettle lost its legs somewhere along the way, so I needed to let it have some air at the bottom to create some updraft for the fire. It works well, and if you have a standard Weber kettle where you can adjust air flow to meet your demands, yours will probably work even better. So, when I describe charcoal grilling in this book, you can imagine it assumes a standard Weber kettle.

Here, then, is a quick primer on the ins and outs of charcoal grilling and gas grilling. Backyard cooking enthusiasts may be stunned that I don't include insulated ceramic charcoal barbecues. The reason isn't because I don't like them (I do like them); it's just that their purpose is tied to their incredible capacity to hold heat with the lid closed. Grilling steak simply doesn't require this capacity; it's faster and more active, requiring just a grill and heat source.

COOKING WITH CHARCOAL

By charcoal I mean hardwood charcoal, or lump charcoal. It has been in use for several thousand years. I avoid charcoal briquettes because they are filled with binders and other compounds, a list of which is never included on their packaging. Lump charcoal also burns hotter than charcoal briquettes, giving the option of cooking at a greater range of temperatures.

Hardwood charcoal, even when it stops smoking, will impart some flavour to your food. Invisible off-gassing compounds continue to occupy the cooking environment even when hardwood charcoal has mostly whitened, or glows orange in the dark. Hardwood charcoal still has enough of its former woody self in it, though the coal is certainly mostly carbon, to impart flavour, and it doesn't take much for us to be able to detect it. Food juices dripping on the coals momentarily cool them, then come back as combusted versions of themselves, now charcoal-kissed with the flavour of combusting lignans, formaldehydes, sugars, and a host of other compounds known generally as polycyclic aromatic compounds (PACs). They taste really good, even if they are not always really good for us.

WHAT'S THE BEST WAY TO LIGHT CHARCOAL?

The best and fastest way to light hardwood charcoal is with a charcoal chimney lighter. A little burning paper in the bottom will start a process that will have your coals ready to go in just a few minutes, not much longer than it takes to heat a gas grill properly.

The other way to light hardwood charcoal is to start a small kindling fire on top of the coals. It takes a bit longer, but the heat will spread and those embers will eventually become one unified heat source.

In either case, avoid chemical accelerants. They tend to get everywhere, and too often that means they're in the food, even if they have long burned off the coals. Once you get your grill heated, let it cool by a third (with some exceptions—I've noted those in specific recipes) before you start cooking your steak. If you can hold your hand 4 inches above the grill (which is already about 4 inches above the coals) for 4 seconds (but only 4 seconds), you're ready to start grilling that steak.

HOW MUCH CHARCOAL SHOULD YOU USE?

It depends on the size of your grill and how long you want it to run hot, but a pile that naturally peaks at 4 inches in the middle, sloping to single nuggets at its perimeter, is ideal. That's about 2 1/2 pounds of charcoal.

HOW HOT DOES CHARCOAL GET?

Hardwood charcoal can reach temperatures of 4,890°F at peak heat, at its surface. Your cooking temperature, another 4 inches or so above the coals, will be 400°F to 500°F once the fire has had a chance to cool a little. Charcoal briquettes max out at 2,300°F at their surface, which means they are considerably cooler at grilling level.

COOKING WITH GAS GRILLS

Not long ago, I was up at our family cabin in the Addington Highlands. The rustic setting includes a fire pit, a Weber kettle barbecue, and in emergencies (for me, anyway) an old propane-fired gas barbecue grill. I planned to be there for a week, and driving up I had visions of cooking all sorts of things on live wood fires. When I got tired of all that stoking and fire management, I figured I would fire up the charcoal kettle. As it turned out, it was a very dry summer and a fire ban was in place, making both of those choices risky and unwise. The gas grill was my only option. As it turned out, it worked perfectly well once I became accustomed to its particularities, and I pulled off some terrific steaks.

HOW HOT DO GAS AND PROPANE GRILLS GET?

Propane flame is 5,072°F. That compares well with the temperature of charcoal or wood flame. So why is it sometimes hard to get the grilling temperatures you want—between 400°F and 500°F—at the grilling surface? It's because there is simply not enough fuel burning at one time to cook food with a lot of direct heat. Even in gas grills with double burners and a great heating plate for extra radiation, heat will dissipate quickly once the hood is open. This is why throughout the recipes I stress the importance of heating the chamber up for 10 minutes on high heat, with the grill hood shut. This heats up the radiating plate and gives the unit more heat inertia for a hotter cooking environment. If you take this precaution, your gas grill should perform well.

CAN I STILL GET SMOKY FLAVOUR?

A great way to add smoky flavour to your food is by slow-burning wood under the grill. To do this, soak your favourite flavouring-wood (wood chips or pellets or just bits of natural wood trimming) in some water, or even in a weak solution of water and brandy, then wrap the wet wood in aluminum foil, punching three or four holes on top, and place it directly on the burner. Shut the hood to enclose your food with the smouldering wood. This smoky event will only last a few minutes, but that's enough to impart significant smoky flavour.

WHAT ABOUT MY BIG GREEN EGG?

If you have a ceramic kamado-style barbecue kit, the recipes for Tri-Tip with Preserved Lemon-Chili Dry Rub and Yogurt Sauce (page 148), Cherry-Grilled Tri-Tip (page 151), and the grilled culotte recipes (pages 113 and 118) work really well, keeping the heat but at lower temperatures. Just grill your steak as you normally would to develop a crust, then close the lid and adjust the venting to turn down the heat. Most of the grilling recipes in this book are optimized for regular gas or charcoal grills. The kamado-style barbecues are adaptable, of course, so you can simply keep the lid open when grilling and use them as you would a charcoal kettle.

PART TWO

THE RECIPES
STEAK BY STEAK

MEET THE

CHUCK

BLADE
(from chuck)

PRIME RIB

FLAT IRON

BRISKET

PETIT
(CLOD)
TENDER

HANGER

WELCOME TO THE MEATY MIDDLE OF THIS BOOK.
All the steaks live here, but as I mentioned in the introduction, our focus is on those somewhat lesser-known cuts: hangers, skirts, bavette, culotte, flank, flat iron, petite tender, and tri-tip. The more you get to know these cuts, the more you can diversify, and I think you will be amazed at how good and how different each cut can be. Big sirloin slices also make an appearance—they are simply too versatile not to include. Rib steak plays a supporting role because it is, quite simply, awesome. Striploin, tenderloin, and porterhouse steaks make delicious cameos, too.

STEAKS

STRIPLOIN
(from short loin)

SHORT LOIN

SIRLOIN

TENDERLOIN

CULOTTE

FLANK

SKIRT

BAVETTE

HANGER

TENDERNESS: moderately tender
GRAIN: loose, coarse, across the width
FAT: moderately fatty
KEY FEATURES: bold taste, very textured, rather engorged

Years ago, on an unseasonably warm day in October, I found myself milling around one of my favourite butcher shops in Toronto, scheming how I might take full advantage of the weather and reawaken my fire pit for one last spectacular grill-up.

I came home with two big hanger steaks, which I'd had only once before, in a restaurant. These two were deeply red and adorned with patches of loose fat, reminding me of the amply fatted lamb meat I would use for traditional souvlaki. Oregano, garlic, grated onion, salt, and lemon juice informed a marinade, and a few hours later I served what I thought was the best souvlaki I had ever tasted: crispy bits of savoury crust and herbal, peppery, juicy chunks of bold-tasting meat.

Hanger steaks are so called because they literally hang off the side of the carcass as it is hung. Whole and untrimmed, they are about the size of a small loaf of bread. By the time we see them in a butcher's case, they are cut lengthwise into two long, floppy steaks, with the tough nerve tissue removed from the middle. They are generally much cheaper than prime cuts, even though there are just two trimmed hangers (four steaks) per animal.

Hanger steaks have large, loose fibres, with the grain running across the steak. At times, I have been surprised by how tender a well-aged hanger steak can be, to the point where I could ignore the direction of the grain and simply grill it with a little salt rub, then slice it willy-nilly or serve it whole. But they are not always that way. A truly tender hanger will yield to your pinch when it is raw, and you could tear it apart easily if you wanted to. Most of the time, though, these steaks are not so soft, and you need to take care to carve them across the grain or tenderize them with a marinade. I don't mind a bit of a chew, but even so, I've been disappointed when I've been inattentive to their particular characters.

The muscle that gives hanger steaks their uniquely bold taste is rather engorged, as hangers are adjacent to a cow's internal organs. This makes the meat prone to poaching and becoming rubbery if grilled too slowly, and the steaks turn out much better when cooked in the dry environment of an open grill rather than pan-fried. The best approach is to cook them on a hot grill until medium-rare. Too rare and hanger steaks will not give up their full potential. Over medium-rare and they become dull and chewy. With these caveats in mind, a properly cooked hanger steak, bursting with rustic, meaty flavour and hearty texture, will inspire you all through the grilling season, right up to the winds of November.

HANGER SOUVLAKI
WITH CHEATER'S TZATZIKI

GRILL

Hanger steaks take remarkably well to marinades, thanks to their loose fibres and extra surface area, which help distribute the marinade through the meat. Since souvlaki portions are chunks instead of slices, marinades serve to tenderize as well as add flavour, just as they do in traditional lamb souvlaki. This marinade also helps the meat retain moisture, so you can cook your souvlaki all the way to medium and enjoy a lovely, dark crust to complement the garlicky "cheater's" tzatziki (there is no need to drain the yogurt, and cucumber is omitted altogether). The flavours and textures in this dish are immensely gratifying, as if matched in the mists of Mount Olympus.

SERVES 2

ZEST AND JUICE OF 1 LEMON
2 LARGE ONIONS, 1 QUARTERED AND 1 GRATED, JUICE RESERVED
1 TABLESPOON DRIED OREGANO
1/2 TEASPOON SALT
FRESHLY GROUND BLACK PEPPER
2 HANGER STEAKS, CUT INTO TWO-BITE CHUNKS

TZATZIKI
1 1/4 CUPS PLAIN FULL-FAT (10% OR HIGHER) GREEK YOGURT
1 TABLESPOON EXTRA-VIRGIN OLIVE OIL
1 CLOVE GARLIC, FINELY GRATED
PINCH OF SALT
FRESHLY GROUND BLACK PEPPER

MARINATE STEAKS: In a bowl or resealable freezer bag, combine lemon zest and juice with grated onion and its juice. Crush oregano between your palms and add to onion mixture. Season with salt and pepper. Add chunks of hanger steak. Turn to coat well. If using a bowl, ensure steak is submerged in liquid and cover. If using a resealable bag, squeeze out air and seal, then slosh meat around until evenly coated. Let sit at room temperature for 30 minutes to 1 hour, or refrigerate for up to 1 day (longer than that and I find the meat becomes too soft).

MAKE CHEATER'S TZATZIKI: In a bowl, combine yogurt, olive oil, garlic, salt, and pepper. Cover and refrigerate for at least 30 minutes to let flavours meld.

ASSEMBLE AND GRILL SOUVLAKI: When nearly ready to grill, gently squeeze meat of some of its marinade (just so it's not soaking wet; be careful not to brush off the bits of onion and lemon zest), then thread somewhat tightly onto metal skewers, alternating each piece with a single layer of quartered onion.

PREPARE YOUR CHARCOAL GRILL to one-third cooler than peak heat, or heat your gas grill to medium-high (preheated on High for 10 minutes, lid closed). Grill souvlaki skewers until they darken and develop a nice crust, and are cooked through to medium.

SERVE with chilled cheater's tzatziki and your choice of side.

CHILI-MARINATED HANGER

GRILL

Sultry and smoky chili gives way to a hint of roasted lime. This is a terrific recipe for a summer's night. Your neighbours will come knocking when they smell this impossibly good steak on the grill. It's especially nice served with Dirty Rice and Beans (page 127).

SERVES 2

3 TABLESPOONS EXTRA-VIRGIN OLIVE OIL
3 TABLESPOONS CHILI POWDER
1 LIME, FOR ZESTING AND JUICING
PINCH OF SALT
1 JALAPEÑO PEPPER, THINLY SLICED
1 BUNCH OF SCALLIONS (ABOUT 5 STALKS),
   THINLY SLICED
2 HANGER STEAKS

COMBINE olive oil, chili powder, lime zest, and salt in a bowl or resealable freezer bag. Add sliced jalapeño and scallions and stir well. Add hanger steaks and turn until well coated. If using a bowl, ensure steak is submerged in liquid and cover. If using a resealable bag, squeeze out air and seal, then slosh meat around until evenly coated. Let sit at room temperature for 30 minutes, or refrigerate for up to 1 day (longer than that and I find the meat becomes too soft).

PREPARE YOUR CHARCOAL GRILL to one-third cooler than peak heat, or heat your gas grill to medium-high (preheated on High for 10 minutes, lid closed). Pat hanger steaks dry with paper towel, and then grill to medium-rare along with the lime (cut in half and grill cut-side down). The steaks should develop a very flavourful, dark crust, and reach an internal temperature approaching 125°F. Take them off the fire and let rest loosely wrapped in foil for 5 minutes.

SLICE THE STEAKS across the grain (almost sideways), and serve with any juices poured overtop and the lime halves for squeezing, as you see fit.

SALTY MARGARITA

This steak goes dangerously well with a salty margarita. My favourite way to make one is the always reliable one-one-one method. Put equal parts fresh lime juice, tequila blanco (100% de agave), and Cointreau in a martini shaker filled with lots of ice cubes. Cover and shake until you feel the ice breaking into smaller bits, and the shaker is cold and frosted. Run the spent half of one of your limes around the rim of a margarita or martini glass, then roll just one side of the glass in a nice medium-coarse sea salt or crumbled Maldon salt. Carefully pour in your margarita mixture. Some of the ice will have disintegrated into tiny shards suspended in the cocktail. Add a few of the larger pieces from the shaker to the glass to keep it cold a little longer, though I've never seen one of these last more than 4 minutes. Garnish with a little bit of lime, if you like.

HANGERS WITH
GRILLED ONIONS AND OLIVE OIL

GRILL

Sausage vendors in Toronto sometimes cook onions on their grills with absolutely no intention of serving them. They do this because the aroma is automatically hunger-inducing. There is definitely something magical about dry cooking an onion, caramelizing the sugars on its surface while maintaining its oniony perfume. The onion becomes partly soft, partly chewy, with just a little crunch. Its dark, sweet-nutty taste melds with the hanger steak to become almost symphonic. This recipe is completely elemental, dead simple, and immensely satisfying at every stage of cooking and eating it.

2 HANGER STEAKS
1 TEASPOON SALT
OLIVE OIL, FOR FRYING
3 LARGE ONIONS, SLICED CROSSWISE
FRESH MINT LEAVES, CHOPPED
FRESH CHIVES, CHOPPED
FRESHLY GROUND BLACK PEPPER

SERVES 2

DUST EACH HANGER STEAK with a little salt (about 1/2 teaspoon per side). Let sit at room temperature for up to 30 minutes before grilling.

PREPARE YOUR CHARCOAL GRILL to one-third cooler than peak heat, or heat your gas grill to medium-high (preheated on High for 10 minutes, lid closed).

RUB EACH STEAK with olive oil, and place on a hot part of the grill. Arrange onion slices (do not rub with oil) as haphazardly as you please around steaks (they won't stick). Cook steaks and onions until they both darken and char a little and the steaks look pinky-red inside, or approach 125°F when tested with a meat thermometer in a meaty section (the steaks will probably be done a minute or two before the onions, which is okay). Let steaks rest loosely wrapped in foil for at least 5 minutes while you finish cooking the onions.

ONCE ONIONS HAVE DARKENED (they won't be done uniformly, and that's perfect), transfer them to a frying pan placed on the grill, reserving the more cooked ones for garnish. Add a splash of olive oil and fry onions lightly for a minute or two, just until softened and starting to sizzle, then scatter over a serving platter.

SLICE YOUR HANGER STEAKS across the grain as best you can, and fan slices over onions on platter. Scatter reserved onions over steak. Season with salt—somewhat less than usual, since you dusted the steaks with salt before grilling them—and sprinkle with chopped mint and chives, and a few twists of pepper. Finish with a stream of olive oil (a tablespoon or more) over the whole thing, and serve.

COOKING WITH OLIVE OIL

I love the rich, grassy flavour of olive oil. I use my best extra-virgin olive oil in so many of my raw recipes (like tzatziki or salad dressing) and marinades. For high-temperature cooking, I will occasionally use olive oil, but not the pricier extra-virgin stuff. Cheaper extra-virgin oils are widely available, and virgin is just fine, and as long as it hasn't expired (check the harvest date, which should be within a year of purchase), that grassy richness will come through, even at higher temperatures. For pan-frying, I mix olive oil with butter, for more flavour and caramelizing power. The oil raises the smoke point of the butter. But I part ways with olive oil when I'm deep-frying (whether in a pan or fryer). For that sort of cooking, I turn to animal fats (but not butter) or, in a pinch, vegetable oils like canola or grapeseed.

ORANGE-SQUEEZED HANGERS WITH QUICK PICKLED PEPPERS

Hanger steaks marinated this way have a sweet-and-sour quality that goes well with plain rice (see recipe page 177) to catch the tangy and joyous flavours of the marinade and lightly pickled peppers.

SERVES 2 TO 4

2 HANGER STEAKS
JUICE OF 5 OR 6 LARGE ORANGES
1 TABLESPOON EXTRA-VIRGIN OLIVE OIL
1 TEASPOON TERIYAKI SAUCE
1 TABLESPOON LIQUID HONEY
1 TEASPOON FRESHLY GRATED PEELED GINGER-ROOT
1 CLOVE GARLIC, FINELY GRATED
PINCH OF CHILI POWDER
1 CUP BREWED SEASONED RICE VINEGAR (APPROX.)
1 CUP COLD WATER (APPROX.)
1 EACH GREEN AND RED BELL PEPPER

USING A SHARP KNIFE, cut each hanger steak in half so you end up with 4 shorter pieces. Place in a bowl with enough orange juice to nearly cover them. Add olive oil, teriyaki sauce, honey, ginger, garlic, and chili powder, and turn until well coated, mixing the marinade as you go. Ensure steaks are completely submerged in liquid, then cover and let sit at room temperature for 1 hour.

MEANWHILE, in a bowl, combine equal parts vinegar and water to make a quick pickle solution and set aside. Cut the peppers in half lengthwise and seed. Cut each half in half again, crosswise, and slice as thinly as you can. Add to vinegar mixture, cover, and refrigerate.

PREPARE YOUR CHARCOAL GRILL to one-third cooler than peak heat, or heat your gas grill to medium-high (preheated on High for 10 minutes, lid closed).

PAT YOUR HANGER STEAKS DRY with paper towel, keeping just enough oil from the marinade on the surface to prevent steaks from clinging to grill.

POUR MARINADE into a fireproof saucepan, and set pan on one side of grill to cook until reduced by one-third. On the other side of the grill, grill your hanger steaks until medium-rare (approaching 125°F when tested with a meat thermometer, or pinky-red in the middle). Set steaks on loose foil and let rest for 4 or 5 minutes, reserving juices.

REMOVE BELL PEPPERS from pickle solution, shake off any excess, and place in a clean bowl. Drizzle with olive oil.

TO SERVE, slice hanger steaks (on a bias across the grain) and divide among the plates. Drizzle with reduced sauce and some of the reserved grilling juices, and garnish with pickled bell peppers.

BUTTER AND HERB-BASTED HANGERS

FRY

Basting steak in a hot pan is as classic a way of cooking as one can get, and I find the activity makes me hungrier as I participate in the steak's journey from raw to done. Since this is a hanger steak, with all its qualities (including its tendency to poach sometimes), I recommend using only the thickest part of the steak, saving the rest for another use, and a heavy pan (cast iron, or with a heat-cookie bottom) wide enough to avoid any crowding—you don't want to see a lot of moisture bubbling away at the bottom of the pan when you're cooking. Done right, which isn't hard, you will end up with a perfectly soft and moist steak baptized with the flavour of herb-infused butter. This goes well with roasted baby potatoes. Another option: sauté some sliced cremini mushrooms until soft and darkened in the same pan you used for the steak (discard the lemon and thyme), tumble them over your steak, and sprinkle with some chopped fresh parsley before serving.

1 OR 2 LARGE HANGER STEAKS
1/2 TEASPOON SALT PER STEAK
UNSALTED BUTTER FOR COOKING
OLIVE OIL, FOR FRYING
1 LEMON, ZESTED AND HALVED CROSSWISE
   (1/2 PER STEAK)
1 BUNCH OF FRESH THYME
FRESHLY GROUND BLACK PEPPER

SERVES 2 TO 4

CUT OUT THE THICKEST PART of the steak (you may have to cut off both ends and save just the thickest part of the middle, depending on the shape). Reserve the rest for another use, like Hanger Souvlaki (see page 57), or freeze for a stew later on. Lightly dust the hanger steak with salt and let sit at room temperature for no less than 30 minutes.

HEAT A HEAVY PAN over medium-high heat. Melt enough butter with olive oil to cover the bottom of the pan by 1/8 inch. Add a few sprigs of thyme and cook just until butter stops bubbling. Add steak along with the cut lemon (unsqueezed). Cook steak to desired doneness (medium-rare works well here), basting with the infused butter as you go. If too much liquid is bubbling in the pan, transfer steak to a side plate, cook pan sauce until it bubbles off, then return steak to the pan. To avoid burning the butter and to help brown the meat, move steak around the pan

often, which will cool the pan and colour the surface of the meat. When the steak is done (approaching 125°F in the middle, or pinky-red when checked with a small incision), let it rest in loose foil for 4 or 5 minutes (reserve the juices). Squeeze lemon into the pan and reserve liquid.

USING A SHARP KNIFE, cut each steak into two or three tidy pieces (which makes for a more tender bite, since cutting a piece through its wider, cut side means you are cutting across the grain in this case). Serve drizzled with some of the foil and pan juices and top each serving with a sprig of thyme and a pinch of lemon zest. Season with salt and pepper, to taste.

PETER SANAGAN'S HERB AND GARLIC-MARINATED HANGER

GRILL

You can catch me cooking up this recipe on any given weekday, thanks to one extraordinary butcher, Peter Sanagan, a trained chef and proud owner of Sanagan's Meat Locker in Toronto's cherished Kensington Market neighbourhood, where I buy them pre-marinated. Peter's formula of herbs and garlic perfectly matches the bold flavour of hanger steak for a lingering soupçon of pine and citrus. You can make the marinade recipe, which I've stolen from his kitchen, way ahead of time. This is great with toast and grilled vegetables, which you can easily make on the same grill while you cook your steak.

AS MANY HANGER STEAKS AS YOU LIKE

MARINADE (PER HANGER STEAK)
3 SPRIGS EACH THYME AND ROSEMARY,
    LEAVES ONLY, CHOPPED
1 CLOVE GARLIC, FINELY GRATED
1/2 TABLESPOON EXTRA-VIRGIN OLIVE OIL
PINCH OF SALT
ZEST AND JUICE OF 1/4 LEMON
FRESHLY GROUND BLACK PEPPER

EACH HANGER SERVES 1 TO 2

USING A MORTAR AND PESTLE, crush thyme, rosemary, and garlic with olive oil and salt until the herbs have broken apart a little and the texture resembles a paste. Add lemon zest and juice and stir well.

IN A BOWL or resealable freezer bag, combine steak and marinade. Turn until well coated, squeezing gently to make sure marinade is in full contact with steak. Let sit at room temperature for 30 minutes to 1 hour, or refrigerate for up to 1 day.

PREPARE YOUR CHARCOAL GRILL to one-third cooler than peak heat, or heat your gas grill to medium-high (preheated on High for 10 minutes, lid closed).

GRILL STEAKS until they colour nicely, as the bits of herbs get dark and sticky. Once they reach an internal temperature approaching 125°F, take them off the fire and let rest loosely wrapped in foil for 5 to 10 minutes.

USING A SHARP KNIFE, cut steak into 1-inch slices. Be sure to cut across the grain, which for hanger steaks is diagonally across their length (see demonstration photos on page 41). Serve the juices from the foil and carving board on the side, in a small dish. Season with pepper to taste.

FLAT IRON

TENDERNESS: quite tender
GRAIN: medium grain runs at a slight angle
through the steak from top to bottom surfaces
FAT: moderately fatty to lean
KEY FEATURES: tender and bouncy texture; easy to slice;
cooks evenly and performs well from rare to medium

The Australians call this truly excellent cut of steak the oyster blade, because it resides just above the centre of the shoulder roll of the cow, underneath the blade bone (scapula), and, like an oyster, is a treasure when it's uncovered. The chuck includes other treasures, like the blade-eye and the petite—or clod—tender, which is detailed later.

The flat iron is narrower and thicker than a flank steak, roughly the size and shape of a cribbage board, tapering at the ends. It's moderately marbled, with a beautiful web of streaky fat on one side. The grain runs mostly from top to bottom through the steak, so an intuitive slice across its width yields a bite that is as tender as can be. Cooked to medium-rare, the flat iron's texture is a little bouncier than a sirloin, and if unadulterated the meat has its own distinct, somewhat veal-like flavour. It can be grilled whole or cut into individual single-serving steaks.

Before being divided into retail steaks, the whole cut of this muscle is separated by a tough tendon running down its centre. This tendon is either removed, giving us the two long, cribbage board–shaped steaks (each good for a meal for four or more hungry people) or left in and cut seven or eight times across, giving us seven or eight small "paleron" steaks, with the tendon in the middle of each. I've bought the whole muscle several times, attempting to remove the central tendon myself. I saved a little money this way, but the job is not as easy as the many hours of instructional videos I watched made it out to be. Now I just let my butcher do it, and pay the extra two dollars a pound—well worth it for this still moderately priced, tremendously good cut of meat. If you don't mind eating around the tendon, then by all means buy the paleron cut for individually portioned steaks.

The flat iron is best cooked medium-rare, but success can be had just under or just over that. Very rare and you may have trouble with the chew. Over medium and you lose the wonderful flavour unique to flat iron. If pressed, I would have to say that the flat iron, properly cooked, is one of the best steak cuts you can buy for the money.

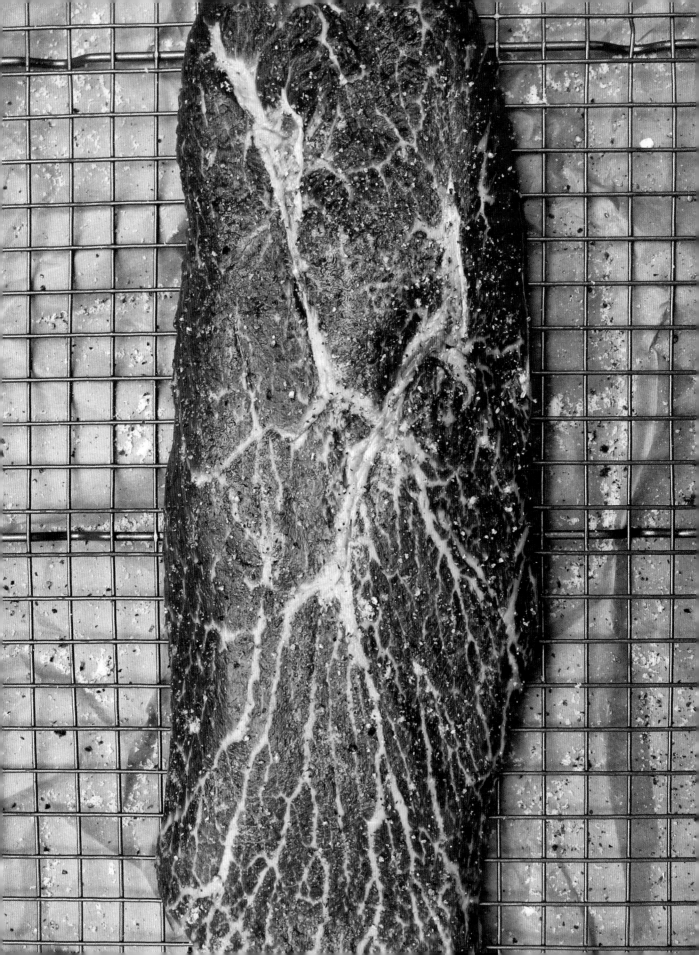

WHOLE FLAT IRON IN FRESH HERBS

GRILL

In the thrill of spring or summer, when a bounty of different fresh herbs are at their plentiful best, this recipe will make you look like a fanciful genius when in fact you'll have hardly done a thing.

SERVES 4

1 BUNCH EACH OF FRESH HERBS: THYME, MINT, TARRAGON, SAGE, CHIVES, ETC., FOR COOKING AND GARNISH

1 WHOLE FLAT IRON STEAK (TENDON REMOVED), ABOUT 2 POUNDS

1 TEASPOON SALT

EXTRA-VIRGIN OLIVE OIL

FRESHLY GROUND BLACK PEPPER

FIRMLY BUT GENTLY RUB sprigs of herbs between your hands or lightly pound them with a potato masher on a cutting board to release the oils and volatile aromatics.

SEASON FLAT IRON with salt (about 1/2 teaspoon per side), and then gently press herbs—stems and all—onto steak (reserve a few herbs for garnish). Drizzle a little olive oil all over. Put steak, surrounded top and bottom in herbs, on a plate. Let sit at room temperature for 30 to 40 minutes before grilling.

PREPARE YOUR CHARCOAL GRILL to one-third cooler than peak heat, or heat your gas grill to medium-high (preheated on High for 10 minutes, lid closed).

PLACE STEAK in its tangle of herbs on grill and cook until medium-rare (approaching 125°F when tested with a meat thermometer, or pinky-red inside with some red meat in the centre when checked with a small incision). Some of the herbs will fall off and land on the coals below, others will sear onto the steak, and some will stick around, only partially cooked—it's all good.

WHEN YOUR STEAK IS DONE, let it rest loosely wrapped in foil for 5 minutes. Transfer the juices to a small bowl, removing any woody bits of herbs.

USING A SHARP KNIFE, slice your flat iron crosswise into 1/4-inch slices. To serve, arrange on a platter, pour reserved juices overtop, sprinkle over remaining herbs, and season with a few grinds of pepper.

WHOLE FLAT IRON WITH SAGE AND LIME

GRILL

Sage and lime both change dramatically when cooked, with the sage practically disappearing, leaving its ghost to wander about with the sultry grilled lime. I use butter to coat the steak and draw these flavours together.

SERVES 4

1 WHOLE FLAT IRON STEAK (TENDON REMOVED)
1 TEASPOON SALT
1 TABLESPOON UNSALTED BUTTER, SOFTENED
1 BUNCH OF FRESH SAGE, LEAVES PICKED
   AND STEMS RESERVED FOR ANOTHER USE
   (SUCH AS STOCK)
1 LIME, HALVED CROSSWISE
FRESHLY GROUND BLACK PEPPER

SEASON YOUR FLAT IRON STEAK with salt (about 1/2 teaspoon per side), and then, using your hands, coat each side with butter (just a light coating; the butter will whiten as you rub it in). Press on as many sage leave as you can to cover each side of the steak. Let sit at room temperature for no longer than 30 to 40 minutes before grilling.

PREPARE YOUR CHARCOAL GRILL to one-third cooler than peak heat, or heat your gas grill to medium-high (preheated on High for 10 minutes, lid closed).

PLACE STEAK, with lime halves alongside, on grill and cook until steak is medium-rare (approaching 125°F when tested with a meat thermometer). Some sage will fall off, and the butter may cause flare-ups, in which case simply move your steak to a cooler part of the grill, remove it until the flare settles, or just let it be if it is momentary.

WHEN YOUR STEAK IS DONE, let it rest loosely wrapped in foil for at least 10 minutes. Transfer the juices to a small bowl.

USING A SHARP KNIFE, slice steak crosswise into 1/4-inch slices. Serve with a lime squeezed on top. Season with pepper to taste.

FLAT IRON WITH
CHILI-LIME SHRIMP, BLISTERED TOMATOES, AND QUESO FRESCO

When my friends return from travelling, I always ask if they had any terrific food experiences. Some find this question perplexing, while others answer right away, excited to share their memories. One such friend, fresh from the island of Santorini in Greece, told me she had eaten roasted tomatoes with shrimp and feta at the same place nearly every day. She found it irresistible, as did I when I cooked what she described, and I made it every couple of weeks for a few months. I inevitably introduced steak to the recipe, and the dish evolved into this delicious bastardization.

SERVES 4

1 FLAT IRON STEAK

PER PERSON
1 TABLESPOON EXTRA-VIRGIN OLIVE OIL
1 TABLESPOON LIQUID HONEY
1/2 TABLESPOON CHILI POWDER
PINCH OF SALT
1 ONION, DIVIDED
1 LIME, HALF FOR JUICING AND HALF FOR GRILLING
4 OR 5 LARGE RAW SHRIMP, PEELED, DEVEINED, AND TAILS INTACT
4 CHERRY TOMATOES
A FEW BASIL LEAVES
3 OUNCES QUESO FRESCO OR FETA CHEESE

IN A LARGE BOWL, combine olive oil, honey, chili, and salt. Lightly coat each side of your flat iron steak with this mixture. Remove steak and let sit at room temperature for no longer than 30 minutes before grilling.

COARSELY GRATE one-third of the onion using the large holes of a box grater (cut the remaining onion into quarters and reserve) and add to the marinade bowl. Add the juice of half a lime and the shrimp. Mix until everything is well coated, then cover and refrigerate for 20 minutes.

MEANWHILE, skewer the cherry tomatoes lengthwise, alternating each with a layer of quartered onion and a basil leaf. Set aside.

AFTER MARINATING the shrimp, thread them onto clean skewers and set aside.

PREPARE YOUR CHARCOAL grill to one-third cooler than peak heat, or heat your gas grill to medium-high (preheated on High for 10 minutes, lid closed).

PLACE STEAK, with the other lime half alongside, on the grill and cook until steak is medium-rare (approaching 125°F when tested with a meat thermometer); a dark, caramel crust should have developed. When your steak is done, remove it and the lime from the grill. Let steak rest loosely wrapped in foil for 5 minutes.

MEANWHILE, place your skewered tomatoes on the grill, followed 2 minutes later by your skewered shrimp. Once the tomatoes blister and char a little, transfer to a side plate. Cook shrimp 2 to 3 minutes, until they are pink and opaque.

USING A SHARP KNIFE, cut steak crosswise into 1/4-inch slices, and transfer to a serving platter. Unload the skewers of shrimp and tomatoes on top. Crumble queso fresco or feta over everything, drop a few torn leaves of basil on top, and then drizzle with olive oil. Dust with a pinch of chili powder and serve.

12-MINUTE FLAT IRON ALL-DAY BREAKFAST

It couldn't be simpler: just pan-fry a piece of flat iron and one egg—that's about 12 minutes to the cure for your hangover or your late-night, worked-too-late hunger pangs, or whatever else might ail you.

SERVES 1

1 PORTION OF FLAT IRON STEAK (6 TO 8 OZ)
1/4 TEASPOON SALT
1 BELL PEPPER (ANY COLOUR YOU LIKE)
2 TABLESPOONS UNSALTED BUTTER, DIVIDED
1/2 TABLESPOON OLIVE OIL, FOR FRYING
1 LARGE EGG
SOURDOUGH OR YOUR FAVOURITE BREAD,
    FOR TOASTING
CRÈME FRAÎCHE OR EXTRA-THICK SOUR CREAM
TABASCO SAUCE
PINCH OF SMOKED PAPRIKA

SPRINKLE both sides of your flat iron steak with salt and set aside.

USING A SHARP KNIFE, cut a wide, flat slice from one of your bell peppers. If it needs more flattening (so that it can lie flush to your pan), press it down against a cutting board with the palm of your hand. Reserve the rest of the pepper for another use.

HEAT a dry non-stick, well-seasoned cast-iron pan or a stainless-steel frying pan over medium-high heat until very hot (you should feel significant heat radiating when you hold your hand 3 inches above the pan's surface). Add 1 tablespoon of butter and the olive oil, and heat until the butter stops bubbling (the oil raises the smoking point of the butter, and helps with the frying).

ADD YOUR FLAT IRON and flat pepper slice to the pan and cook steak until medium-rare (approaching 125°F when tested with a meat thermometer, or pinky-red inside when checked with a small incision), moving it around the pan and flipping it as often as you

like; cook the pepper until softened and the skin side is a bit blackened. Transfer the pepper to a side dish. Let steak rest loosely wrapped in foil while you complete the next steps.

WIPE THE PAN with a paper towel and return the pan to medium-high heat. Melt 1 tablespoon butter, and then fry your egg. Cover the pan with a lid to whiten the yolk coating. The moment the surface of the yolk has whitened, remove pan from the heat and set aside, uncovered. While the egg is frying in the residual heat, toast your bread.

TO SERVE, spread a good amount of crème fraîche on the toast and add a dash of Tabasco. Top with the pepper slice (cut-side up), the flat iron steak, a little more crème fraîche, and another dash of Tabasco. Finish with the fried egg and a dusting of paprika. Dig in and enjoy.

COMPOUND BUTTER

Compound butter isn't just flavoured butter (like garlic butter) but exquisitely and expressly flavoured butter meant to accompany food, especially steak (fish and pasta, too!). Rather than melting the butter with flavourings, flavours are pounded into hard butter, which expels some of the butter's moisture, leaving the butter more fat-concentrated and supremely textured. I've provided some herb-and-spice combinations that have worked well for me (see photo caption on page 79).

When using spices, it's best to lightly toast them in a dry pan before grinding them (it really brings their flavours to the surface). You can toast pre-ground spices, too, but not as effectively—keep an eye on them; they will toast very quickly. When using fresh herbs, mince the herbs as finely as you can before pounding them into the butter.

Making compound butter is a messy and wholly gratifying experience, and the butter will keep for weeks in the fridge and much longer in the freezer.

MAKES 1 LOG OF COMPOUND BUTTER

1/2 cup unsalted butter, fridge hard

3/4 teaspoon salt

Flavourings of your choice (about 1 tablespoon dried spices
    or about 1 cup loosely packed fresh herbs)

On a cutting board, pound butter and salt into your flavouring(s) with your palms or a potato masher. Using your hands, fold and squeeze it until everything is fully incorporated (you will almost certainly wring some moisture from the butter, and that's good). Working quickly, before the butter melts too much in your hands, shape it into a log. Wrap it in plastic wrap, and freeze or refrigerate.

When you're ready to use it, let compound butter sit at room temperature for a minute or two, until it's a little softer than fridge hard, and then cut it into 1/4-inch slices. Place a medallion on top of your steak, where it will melt its way to splendid harmony.

FLAT IRON FOR ONE,
WITH SCALLION COMPOUND BUTTER AND CREMINI MUSHROOMS

I love the efficiency of starting with just a few simple ingredients and using the whole of them. You can make this dish anytime, but it's even better when you can find true spring onions. I've also used ramps (a.k.a. wild leeks) to make the compound butter (pictured here).

There is a satisfying amount of pounding, chopping, and squeezing to this recipe. If you're disappointed by everything that has happened to you so far today, this will set things straight, and you get leftover compound butter as a bonus, which you can save for pasta, toast, or steak another time.

1 FLAT IRON STEAK (6 TO 8 OUNCES)
1/4 TEASPOON SALT
1 BUNCH OF SPRING ONIONS, SCALLIONS, OR RAMPS
1/2 CUP UNSALTED BUTTER, FRIDGE HARD
1 TABLESPOON OLIVE OIL, FOR FRYING
3 CREMINI MUSHROOMS, SLICED
FRESHLY GROUND BLACK PEPPER

SERVES 1

SPRINKLE both sides of your flat iron steak with salt. Let sit while you make the compound butter.

USING A SHARP KNIFE, trim your spring onions, cutting off the roots and any wilted or damaged green parts. Cut the white part of the stalks away from the greens, then cut the white stalks in half so you end up with two 1-inch sections of white stalks (about 12 pieces total per bunch); set the whites aside. Chop the greens as finely as you can, then sprinkle with a pinch of salt and continue chopping until almost minced.

RESERVE 2 tablespoons of butter for later. On a cutting board, using your palms or a potato masher, pound the rest of the butter into the chopped spring onion greens. Scrape the butter from the board, folding it and squeezing it with your hands until everything is fully incorporated (you will almost certainly wring some moisture from the butter, and that's good). Before the butter melts too much in your hands, quickly shape it into a log. Wrap it in plastic wrap, and refrigerate.

IN A HEAVY FRYING PAN over medium-high heat, melt 1 tablespoon of the reserved butter with olive oil, and heat until the butter stops bubbling. Fry your flat iron steak until it develops a nice crust and reaches medium-rare (approaching 125°F when tested with a meat thermometer, or pinky-red inside when checked with a small incision), flipping it as often as you like and moving it around the pan. Let it rest loosely wrapped in foil while you cook the remaining onions.

ADD prepared white onion to the pan along with the remaining tablespoon of reserved butter, the sliced mushrooms, and a small pinch of salt. Sauté until the onions and mushrooms have softened and started to darken, then remove from heat.

SERVE your flat iron scattered with the sautéed mushrooms and onions, and a generous slice of compound butter on top. Season with ground pepper to taste.

PETITE (CLOD) TENDER

TENDERNESS: very tender
GRAIN: fine grain runs along the length
FAT: very lean
KEY FEATURES: delicate meat; loses moisture quickly when
cooked; does well cooked to rare; handsome shape, great for slicing

The petite tender, sometimes called a clod tender or mock tenderloin, is one of the most tender beef cuts you can get. Each petite tender is a single muscle, which the butcher seams out of the centre of the shoulder roll. This muscle doesn't do a lot of work for the live animal; it's mostly responsible for coordinating movements between other muscles. The petite tender tastes mild and is very lean, and it can quickly dry out if cooked beyond rare. I sometimes think of it as the boneless chicken breast of beef.

Even though these traits may not sound like advantages, this often-ignored cut has its merits: The meat is truly uniformly graded; its already tender fibres run conveniently along its length for easy across-the-grain slicing. It is about the size and shape of a croissant, perfect for carving handsome slices and serving convenient portions. It is also often much cheaper than other steaks, even though there are only two of them per beast.

The best way to enjoy petite tenders is to cook them only until rare, leaving them red (quite red, if you can) and just warm in the middle. It is also a good steak to serve cold and sliced for lunch (and you can cook it past rare for that). With a little care, these peculiar-looking steaks can be made into dishes that are truly surprising and special.

CHARRED TERIYAKI PETITE TENDER

GRILL

One night after work, I had the great pleasure of sitting down for a meal with Jamie Oliver to discuss his latest cookbook. We went to Bar Isabel, a popular Spanish-style restaurant in Toronto owned by chef Grant van Gameren. Among the plates was a splendid sliced steak, the darkest brown on the outside yet warm and red on the inside. Masterfully caramelized, salty, with a toffee-like coating, the velvety rare beef was succulent. The cut was striploin, but I thought to myself right then and there that this sort of treatment would be perfect for petite tenders. I was way too distracted by the food and conversation (and maybe the wine) to ask the chef how he'd prepared the steak, so I spent the following weekend trying to figure it out. This recipe is as close as I could get, and it's now part of my steak repertoire.

1 TABLESPOON UNSALTED BUTTER

1 TABLESPOON TERIYAKI SAUCE

1 TABLESPOON RED PEPPER PASTE OR TOMATO PASTE

1 TABLESPOON LIQUID HONEY

ZEST OF 1 LEMON

2 TEASPOONS FRESH LEMON JUICE

1 CLOVE GARLIC, FINELY GRATED

1 PETITE TENDER STEAK (ABOUT 12 OUNCES)

SERVES 1 TO 2

IN A SMALL SAUCEPAN over medium heat, heat butter until it just stops bubbling. Add teriyaki sauce, red pepper paste, honey, lemon zest and juice, and garlic. Simmer over medium-low heat until thickened slightly, about 2 minutes. Remove pan from the heat and set aside until the marinade has cooled. Transfer to a bowl or resealable freezer bag.

ADD YOUR PETITE TENDER to the cooled marinade and turn the steak until it is well coated. Let sit for 30 minutes, or more if you can—your petite tender will be on the grill for just a short amount of time, so you want it to soak in a good amount of flavour. This should also give you enough time to prepare your grill.

PREHEAT YOUR GRILL to its hottest setting: peak heat for charcoal grills; full-on high heat for gas grills (with the hood or lid closed for about 10 minutes to heat up the plating). When your gas grill temperature reads in excess of 500°F or your charcoal grill is too hot to hold your hand 4 inches above the grill for much more than a second, and the coals have just turned mostly white, with scant streaks of black, it's time to start cooking (see "Cooking with Charcoal," pages 47–48, for more on this subject).

REMOVE YOUR STEAK from the marinade and pat off any excess, leaving just enough to coat.

PLACE THE MARINATED PETITE TENDER on the hottest part of your grill, and cook until it darkens, turning as needed to develop a nice, even crust. You are looking for a crust that is very dark brown and black over the surface of the whole steak, except for any small patches where the coating may have rubbed off. If you are using an instant-read thermometer, cook steak to an internal temperature of 100°F, but no higher. If you don't have a thermometer, cut a small incision into the middle of the steak and test it with your finger; inside it should be red and soft but quite warm to the touch. You should find that the crust will tell most of the story: when it is dark and beautiful, the steak is very likely perfectly cooked.

WHEN YOUR STEAK IS DONE, transfer it to a cutting board and let rest for 5 minutes. Using a sharp knife, cut it crosswise into 1/8-inch slices. To serve, fan the slices out on a plate like fallen dominoes. Put the plate in front of your guests and watch your perfectly cooked petite tender disappear.

OLIVE-STUFFED PETITE TENDER PICNIC SLICES

FRY

Cooked all the way to medium, petite tenders are tender enough to serve cold as sliced luncheon meat. I've stuffed them with chopped spicy green olives here, but you can stuff them any way you like. Just remember that whatever you use won't cook all that much inside the steak, so you will want your stuffing ready to go, or cooked beforehand. It's important to wait until the steak has cooled in the fridge for at least 2 hours to help the flavours meld and so that the steak is the right consistency for slicing. The result: a perfectly tasty item for a snack, hors d'oeuvre, picnic, or sandwich.

Note that you can work with the petite tender directly from the fridge (in fact, it's a little easier to work with cold meat in this instance).

AS MANY PETITE TENDER STEAKS AS YOU LIKE

PER PETITE TENDER
2 TABLESPOONS FINELY CHOPPED SPICY GREEN
    DELI OLIVES
1 TABLESPOON DRIED HERBES DE PROVENCE
PINCH OF SALT
1 TABLESPOON OLIVE OIL, FOR FRYING
FRESHLY GROUND BLACK PEPPER

EACH PETITE TENDER SERVES 1 TO 2

USING A SMALL BONING KNIFE, gently poke a tunnel through the steak from end to end. Carefully twist the knife around to enlarge the hole a little, or use the handle of a wooden spoon (the tunnel will widen to roughly 1/4 inch in diameter, or more when fully stuffed). Stuff the steak with the chopped olives, and set aside.

SPRINKLE a clean work surface with the herbes de Provence and salt, then roll the stuffed steak in the seasoning, being careful to coat it evenly. Set aside.

HEAT OLIVE OIL in a heavy frying pan over medium heat until really hot (the oil will thin in the pan, and sizzle when tested with a drop of water). Place prepared steak in the pan and cook until it reaches medium (about 130°F to 135°F when tested with an instant-read thermometer, or firm and ever-so-slightly pink when tested by a small, careful incision), about 7 minutes, depending on your pan and stovetop. Some of the stuffing will leak out of the steak, but this just makes things that much more scrumptious. Transfer the steak to a plate and let rest for 10 minutes or until cool enough to handle.

SEASON cooled steak with a few grinds of pepper, and then wrap snugly in plastic wrap and refrigerate until cold and firm, at least 2 hours or up to 1 day.

USING A VERY SHARP KNIFE, cut the steak crosswise into smooth, even slices, a little more than a 1/4 inch thick.

QUICK PICKLES

Quick vinegar pickles are so easy to make, and if you get the acid and sweetness just right, they are a perfectly fantastic way to preserve the seasonal harvest. Quick pickles last for at least a month in the fridge. I often bring mine out to add a little tang and crunch to steak lunches and dinners. They make a perfect addition to a picnic, too.

WHITE WINE VINEGAR
WATER
PEPPERCORNS
SUGAR
SALT
MEDIUM PICKLING CUCUMBERS
  (KIRBY CUCUMBERS WORK WELL)
ONION, CUT INTO WEDGES
GARLIC CLOVES, HALVED
DILL FLOWER OR DILL SEEDS (OPTIONAL)

FILL CLEAN 1-PINT (500 mL) mason jars with hot tap water and set aside while you prepare the pickles. (Mason jars with "shoulders" are preferable, so that the pickles won't all float to the top.)

IN A SAUCEPAN, heat equal parts vinegar and water along with peppercorns (about 5 per jar) until the brine just begins to boil. Add a little sugar and salt, to taste. Taste and adjust vinegar, sugar, and/or salt, if necessary.

EMPTY MASON JARS of water, then stuff in as many cucumbers as you can fit in each jar (halve or quarter some of the cucumbers lengthwise if needed), along with 1 to 2 onion wedges, 2 garlic cloves, and 1 whole dill flower or 1 tablespoon dill seeds (if using).

POUR IN BRINE, including peppercorns, until cucumbers are completely covered, leaving 1 inch headspace.

COVER WITH SNAP lids and secure rings until just fingertip tight. Let sit at room temperature for 30 minutes or until the jars are lukewarm or cooler to the touch, then refrigerate for at least 24 hours before serving.

CARPACCIO WITH
BEET-PICKLED MANDARIN ORANGE

. . . .

When preparing raw meat dishes like carpaccio or tartar, there is all the more reason to use high-quality, fresh meat. Both you and your guests should be just as confident in your carpaccio as your grilled steak. Carpaccio is not meant to be filling. It's like a perfectly wonderful, short conversation: vibrant, enlightening, and then over. Petite tenders are indeed tender enough for carpaccio, and I think perform even better than tenderloin in this case. You can take carpaccio in many directions. Some recipes emphasize indulgence and rich flavours. I've gone the other way here: earthy and refreshing. When you achieve the right balance of flavour, consistency, and presentation, a great plate of carpaccio will let your dinner guests know they are in good hands. Serve the carpaccio on its own or with a nice baguette and some olive oil for drizzling.

1 SMALL MANDARIN ORANGE OR CLEMENTINE
    (UNPEELED)
1 SHALLOT
1/2 CUP PICKLED BEET BRINE (APPROX.)
OLIVE OIL, FOR FRYING
1 PETITE TENDER STEAK
5 TO 6 CAPERS PER SERVING OF CARPACCIO,
    EXCESS BRINE GENTLY SQUEEZED OUT
1 LEMON (1/2 FOR ZESTING AND JUICING,
    1/2 SLICED FOR GARNISH)
SALT AND PEPPER

SERVES 6 TO 8 AS AN APPETIZER

. . . .

USING A SHARP KNIFE, cut mandarin orange lengthwise, as thinly as you can, into very thin slices (top to bottom, with the grain, to get tidier, sturdier slices). Cut shallot crosswise, as thinly as you can, into rings. Transfer orange and shallot to a bowl, cover with beet brine, and refrigerate until chilled.

HEAT A HEAVY PAN over high heat. Add just enough olive oil to coat the bottom of the pan. When the oil starts to shimmer, sear your petite tender on all sides for just a few seconds, until the entire surface loses its pinkness. This adds a nice outline to your carpaccio and takes care of any surface microbes (you are not looking for a crust here, and the steak is still very much raw).

LET SEARED STEAK COOL for a minute, then wrap tightly in plastic wrap. Transfer to the freezer for 20 minutes or until the steak firms up considerably but is not actually frozen (this will make it easier to slice).

USING A SHARP CHEF'S KNIFE, cut prepared steak in half crosswise. Starting from the cut end, slice it, as thinly as you can, into medallions. One at a time, place each medallion between two sheets of plastic wrap. Using a kitchen mallet or a blunt potato masher (the kind without holes), pound meat firmly but not brutally, thinning it and expanding the diameter of the slice between the plastic wrap. Try to get the thinness as even as possible, and don't worry too much about the actual shape of the slice or if it has a few holes in it.

PEEL THE SHEETS of carpaccio (which should be thin, almost see-through, and even somewhat lacy) from the plastic and arrange over a chilled serving plate. Sprinkle with capers. Top with beet-pickled oranges and shallots, a drizzle of olive oil, a little lemon zest and squirt of lemon juice, a sprinkle of salt, and a grind or two of black pepper. Garnish with a slice of lemon.

TIP: I love this version of carpaccio served with an absolutely freezing-cold shot of aquavit in a frozen shot glass. If you don't have aquavit, put a bottle of nice vodka in the freezer for 2 hours (or just keep it there all the time), along with some single shot glasses. When you are ready to serve, bring out the glasses, pour in the spirits, and then zest a bit of lemon overtop and finish with a grind of pepper.

HOW TO MAKE QUICK PICKLED BEETS

If you don't have a jar of pickled beets in the fridge, it's easy to make some pickled beet brine. Place 1 large beet and enough water to cover it in a saucepan over medium-low heat. Add 1/2 teaspoon salt and a few whole black peppercorns. Bring to a boil, and then simmer for 20 minutes or until the beet is tender but still a bit firm (when tested with a fork, you should feel even resistance all the way through to the centre). Let the beet cool slightly, then cut into bite-size wedges. Place in a 1-pint (500 mL) mason jar with equal parts white vinegar and your brewed beet water (including the peppercorns). Add 1 teaspoon granulated sugar and stir well. Taste the brine and add more sugar or salt, to taste, along with some onion slices. Cover and refrigerate. It will last for at least a month in the fridge, unless you eat it all first.

PETITE TENDER MEDALLIONS WITH
FRESH HERBS AND LEMON CREAM

The inspiration for this recipe comes from years of watching and reading about legendary Parisian butcher Hugo Desnoyer. He has achieved god-like status in France, and for good reason. His approach to meat, beef in particular, is something to be respected and emulated. One of his mantras, "*C'est l'herbe qui donne le goût à la viande*," is an outlook that I deeply believe in: the taste of meat is flavoured by what the cow has eaten throughout its life. Desnoyer knows steak like no one else, and his recipes are built from the steak up, not the other way around, always complementing and taking full advantage of a steak's particular character. This straightforward recipe is my own, but in a daydream I imagine Monsieur Desnoyer across the table, fork in hand, having just taken a bite, nodding approval in my direction.

This preparation takes complete advantage of the petite tender: the cut is lean and pale compared to other steaks, so the creamy, lemony sauce embraces it wonderfully. It involves nearly no cooking time, since you are simply searing the sliced medallions to bring the meat to just over rare. Use the nicest fresh, tender herbs you can find.

2 PETITE TENDER STEAKS

PER PETITE TENDER
1 TABLESPOON UNSALTED BUTTER
2 TABLESPOONS OLIVE OIL, FOR FRYING
1 LEMON, FOR ZESTING AND JUICING
SPLASH OF DRY WHITE WINE
4 TABLESPOONS HEAVY OR WHIPPING (35%) CREAM
PINCH OF SALT
2 TABLESPOONS CRÈME FRAÎCHE
2 TO 3 SPRIGS OF FRESH THYME (OR YOUR FAVOURITE HERBS), FINELY CHOPPED, WITH SOME NICE LEAVES RESERVED
FRESHLY GROUND BLACK PEPPER

SERVES 2 AS A MAIN DISH OR MORE AS AN APPETIZER

USING A SHARP chef's or butcher's knife, slice your petite tender into tidy medallions, about 3/4 inch thick. Set aside.

HAVE A WARM PLATE at the ready. In a stainless-steel or non-stick pan (with a heat-cookie bottom) over medium-high heat, melt butter with olive oil and heat until the butter nearly stops bubbling. Place your petite tender medallions in the pan (being careful not to overcrowd) and quickly sear both sides for about 1 minute per side; they won't colour much at all, but the inside of your medallions should be fully warm and rare in the middle. (Try first cooking a single piece to practise—one of the less attractive slices—to get this part right.) Transfer cooked medallions to the warmed plate, reserving the pan over the heat.

REDUCE THE HEAT to medium-low, then add the juice of slightly less than half the lemon to the pan along with a splash of white wine. Cook until the pan juices are reduced by one-third, stirring with a wooden spoon to scrape up any browned bits at the bottom of the pan (there won't be that much to deglaze). Add cream, salt, crème fraîche, chopped herbs, and two fine grates of lemon zest (use a Microplane or fine-tooth grater), stir well, and cook until thickened, about 3 minutes. Once the sauce reaches a consistency you like (add more cream or crème fraîche, if needed), neatly pour some over the steak medallions. Grind some pepper overtop, sprinkle with the reserved herb leaves and another fine grating of lemon zest, and raise a little glass to Monsieur Desnoyer.

TOP SIRLOIN SLICE

TENDERNESS: moderately tender
GRAIN: densely packed, fine grain runs through the steak, top to bottom surface
FAT: moderately fatty to lean, often sold with a hard fat cap left intact
KEY FEATURES: versatile and takes well to a grill and a frying pan

---

The top sirloin part of beef can be divided into many steaks, but the one I like the best, and one that is quite commonly on offer in butcher shops and grocery stores, is the top sirloin slice. This generally includes a cross-section of the gluteus medius and biceps femoris muscles, near the hip. It is right in the middle in terms of tenderness, and for the price I find it to be highly versatile and quite forgiving, lending itself equally well to the three major steak cooking methods in this book: grilling, pan-frying, and reverse-searing.

One can often see top sirloins on sale, cut into single-serving steaks. I like buying the whole piece, though, since I can control the thickness that way, cutting it into portions myself, as I see fit. Its dense grain runs top to bottom through the steak, as well as along its length, depending on what part is cut. It is easy enough to slice for tenderness in any case, and there are certainly many great ways to take advantage of the top sirloin's all-purpose view on life as a steak.

TOP SIRLOIN WITH LEMON AND OREGANO

REVERSE-SEAR

In this recipe, oregano is used to season the meat as part of what I call a deconstructed marinade. The taste is fresh and satisfying, and the recipe is certainly easy enough to pull off on a work day or as part of a bigger, more complicated weekend dinner plan. I eat sirloin this way a lot, but it always feels special to me.

SERVES 4 TO 6

1 TEASPOON DRIED OREGANO FLORETS OR COARSE DRIED OREGANO

1 WHOLE TOP SIRLOIN STEAK, AT LEAST 1 INCH THICK (ABOUT 2 POUNDS)

1 TEASPOON SALT, OR TO TASTE

UNSALTED BUTTER AND OLIVE OIL, FOR FRYING

1/2 LEMON, ZESTED (RESERVE LEMON FOR JUICING)

2 CLOVES GARLIC, HALVED OR QUARTERED, DEPENDING ON SIZE

4 SHALLOTS, QUARTERED OR CUT INTO EIGHTHS, DEPENDING ON SIZE

FRESHLY CRACKED BLACK PEPPER

PLACE A WIRE RACK on the middle rack of the oven and line the rack below it with enough foil to catch the steak drippings while allowing the steak to bask freely in your oven's dry winds. There won't be much dripping, but this makes cleanup easy and will ensure you don't get a smoky oven the next time you cook at higher temperatures. Preheat your oven to 225°F.

PLACE OREGANO in the palm of your hand and briefly rub hands together to release the oil in the leaves. Gently pat evenly onto each side of the steak. Generously season each side with salt (about 1/2 teaspoon per side).

PLACE YOUR SEASONED SIRLOIN on the wire rack in your preheated oven, and cook for 30 minutes per pound, turning once halfway through to dry out both sides evenly, until it reaches an internal temperature of 115°F in the middle (that is, not in a seam or in fat, but in the meatiest part of the middle of the steak).

MEANWHILE, about 5 minutes before your steak is ready, place a heavy pan (cast iron or stainless steel are best, or use a non-stick pan with a heat-cookie bottom) over high heat and heat until very hot.

WHEN YOUR SIRLOIN IS READY, remove it from the oven and rub one side generously with butter. Carefully add a splash of olive oil to the hot pan and sear steak, buttered-side down first. Wait 30 seconds, and then flip, searing the other side of the steak, flipping again as needed until a nice, dark brown crust develops and the steak reaches an internal temperature approaching 125°F in the middle. Then, sprinkle the steak evenly with half of the lemon zest. Transfer the steak to a sheet of foil (keep the pan on the heat), wrap very loosely, and let rest.

REDUCE THE HEAT to medium, and add garlic and shallots to the reserved pan. Place zested lemon half cut-side down in the pan alongside garlic and shallots. Once lemon is lightly browned and feels soft enough to squeeze very easily, remove it from the pan and reserve it for later. Continue cooking the garlic and shallots until softened and slightly browned. (This should take about 4 minutes, total.)

SERVE YOUR SIRLOIN on a platter or right on your carving board, cut into 1/2-inch slices, cutting across the width. Scatter softened shallots and garlic overtop, and add a squeeze of the warmed lemon (to taste) and a grind of pepper. To finish, sprinkle with some of the remaining lemon zest.

TOP SIRLOIN WITH GRILLED-ON SCALLIONS

GRILL

I've used garlic chives here but this steak is equally delicious grilled with scallions—just make sure to chop them finely so they are light enough to stick to steak. Whichever you choose, the result is a delicious steak bejewelled with flavour.

SERVES 4 TO 6

1 SIRLOIN SLICE, ABOUT 1 1/2 INCHES THICK
   (ABOUT 2 POUNDS)
1 TEASPOON SALT
UNSALTED BUTTER, SOFTENED
1 BUNCH OF SCALLIONS (ABOUT 5 STALKS)
   OR GARLIC CHIVES, FINELY CHOPPED
FRESHLY GROUND BLACK PEPPER

SEASON YOUR SIRLOIN steak with salt (about 1/2 teaspoon per side). Let rest for no longer than 30 to 40 minutes before grilling.

USING YOUR HANDS, lather a knob of butter evenly onto each side of the steak. Coat each side with as much of the chopped scallions as you can, pressing them in a little with your hands. Set aside.

PREPARE YOUR CHARCOAL GRILL to one-third cooler than peak heat, or heat your gas grill to medium-high (preheated on High for 10 minutes, lid closed). Grill sirloin until a nice, dark brown crust forms and it reaches medium (approaching 125°F when tested with a meat thermometer, or pinky-red inside when checked with a small incision). The butter will help the scallions stick to the steak, though you will lose some to the grill. Let rest loosely wrapped in foil for about 5 minutes.

USING A SHARP KNIFE, cut steak into 1/4-inch slices and devour.

WICKING

"Wicking" may be a term that I've coined, but the process is certainly recognized. When a steak's grain runs vertically from the grilling or frying surface (as in a sirloin slice) moisture can wick out of the steak and onto the coals or into the pan more quickly than with a steak with a horizontal grain (like a bavette or skirt steak). This is because the fibres have been cut short already, and there is simply less space inside the steak for the juices to go when under pressure from cooking. For this reason, you may want to remove these cuts from the heat a bit earlier than your instant-read thermometer might indicate (4°F earlier should do the trick), or double check your steak for doneness by making a small incision with a knife a minute or two before you think the steak might be done.

TERIYAKI TOP SIRLOIN
WITH SPROUTS AND MUSHROOMS

Teriyaki is a quintessential Japanese way of cooking, specifically created for grilling. Its origins date back to the 17th century, and it has enjoyed widespread adoration ever since. The sauce, made by reducing fermented soy sauce with sake and honey, adds flavour and creates a sort of glaze that develops an insanely unctuous crust on grilled foods. Its umami character supercharges savoury flavours, which, in the case of steak, will lead to desperate cries for more from your guests.

If you have a favourite brand of teriyaki sauce, by all means use it, but if you're unfamiliar with its charms, I recommend buying a bottle of Kikkoman teriyaki sauce. It's widely available and has maintained a standard of high quality for a really long time. I've added an extra few ingredients to the crust of the steak so it's bursting with flavour, and so you will truly appreciate the tremendous versatility of top sirloin.

SERVES 4 TO 6

1 TOP SIRLOIN SLICE, ABOUT 1 1/2 INCHES THICK (ABOUT 2 POUNDS)

1 TEASPOON LIQUID HONEY

1 CLOVE GARLIC, FINELY GRATED

2 THUMBS OF FRESH PEELED GINGERROOT, 1 PURÉED AND 1 CUT INTO MATCHSTICKS

1 CUP TERIYAKI SAUCE

JUICE OF 1/4 LIME

1/2 TEASPOON JAPANESE RICE VINEGAR

FAT, FOR FRYING (TALLOW, LARD, DUCK FAT, OR BUTTER WITH A LITTLE OLIVE OIL)

1 MEDIUM ONION, HALVED AND THEN SLICED THINLY WITH THE GRAIN

1 CUP EACH SLICED CREMINI AND SHIITAKE MUSHROOMS

2 CUPS BEAN SPROUTS, DIVIDED

PINCH OF ALEPPO OR KOREAN GOCHUGARU PEPPER

1/2 BUNCH OF SCALLIONS (ABOUT 3 STALKS), THINLY SLICED

USING YOUR HANDS, evenly coat the steak with honey, then rub on finely grated garlic and puréed ginger. Transfer to a resealable freezer bag and add teriyaki sauce, lime juice (toss in squeezed lime as well), and rice vinegar. Seal bag, give it a good turn or two to mix the marinade, and let sit at room temperature for at least 1 hour or refrigerate for up to 1 day.

PREPARE YOUR CHARCOAL GRILL to one-third cooler than peak heat, or heat your gas grill to medium-high (preheated on High for 10 minutes, lid closed). Grill your steak (reserve marinade) until it reaches an internal temperature of 125°F, or looks pinky-red inside when checked with a small incision. Set aside very loosely wrapped in foil.

IN A PAN SUITABLE FOR THE GRILL (cast iron and stainless steel are best, or use a high-quality pan with a heat-cookie bottom and metal handle), fry sliced onion and mushrooms and matchsticks of ginger in your fat of choice until the onions begin to soften and mushrooms find their sheen, about 4 minutes. Then add half the bean sprouts and 3 tablespoons of the reserved marinade (discard the rest). Cook for about a minute longer, just until the sprouts wilt.

USING A SHARP KNIFE, slice steak into attractive, manageable pieces and arrange on a serving platter. Spoon the onion and mushroom mixture on top, and sprinkle with sliced scallions and the remaining sprouts.

SAKE SANGRIA

The perfect liquid prelude to teriyaki:
Mix 1 ounce each dry sake and red wine
with 4 ounces lemon–lime soda. Serve over
ice, garnished with slivers of apple.

PORTERHOUSE, STRIPLOIN, AND TENDERLOIN

TENDERNESS: striploin is really tender;
tenderloin is even more tender; porterhouse comprises both
GRAIN: grain runs through the steaks from top to bottom surface
FAT: striploin is moderately to amply fatty with a hard fat cap generally
left intact; tenderloin is leaner; porterhouse combines both of these things
KEY FEATURES: Striploin has an even bite and fine texture, and AAA or
prime grades are well marbled with fat. Nicely shaped for slicing, they are
fast-cooking and have a medium, beefy flavour. Tenderloin is absolutely
tender, and quite mild tasting if left on its own. It performs well from quite
rare to medium-rare. Porterhouse is in fact a striploin and a tenderloin,
separated by a T-bone-shaped cross-section of the chine bone.
It rivals rib steak in its outright awesomeness.

Striploin, tenderloin, and porterhouse are, let's face it, steak royalty. They are tender and easy to cook, cooking quickly (and losing moisture quickly, too), as the grain is fine and short because of the way it is cut. Tenderloin on its own will take a little longer to get to medium-rare than a striploin because it is more engorged. When both steaks are still attached to the bone as a porterhouse, I find that they cook at roughly the same rate, the tenderloin catching up to the striploin because of the greater surface area that the striploin has in contact with the backbone (chine bone).

Striploin and tenderloin are wonderful grilled or fried. Porterhouse works better on a grill because the bone can interfere with the meat making full and constant contact with the hot pan. A true porterhouse is cut from the cross-section of the backbone toward the rear of the cow. The meat is more tender here, and the tenderloin (or filet mignon) is larger. Further toward the front of the cow, porterhouse becomes T-bone, and even further up it becomes club steak.

I've included just a sprinkling of recipes here because, as I've mentioned, our focus remains with the many other cousins in this extended family, and because these highly prized (and priced) steaks need very little done to them. The tenderloin is on the mild side, and benefits from a boost of fat and smoke, and there are easy, tasty fixes for that.

PORTERHOUSE
(full steak)

STRIPLOIN

TENDERLOIN

CARVED PORTERHOUSE OF THE GODS

I find such joy in cooking steak on the bone—and here we have a big steak with a big bone. You'll find there are so many impressive aspects to this steak that it needs very little done to it. The art, along with just-right cooking, of course, is in how the steak is carved and presented. You'll be rewarded by the look of sheer delight on your guests' faces. If you want them to call the vice squad or change religions, have some Stilton cheese on the side for crumbling overtop.

1 BIG PORTERHOUSE STEAK (ABOUT 2 INCHES THICK)
1 TEASPOON SALT
UNSALTED BUTTER, SOFTENED
FRESHLY GROUND BLACK PEPPER

SERVES 4 TO 6

SEASON YOUR PORTERHOUSE steak with salt (about 1/2 teaspoon per side). Let sit at room temperature for at least 30 minutes, preferably longer, and up to 2 hours. Using your hands, rub a little butter on just one side of the steak, lathering it evenly.

PREPARE YOUR CHARCOAL GRILL to one-third cooler than peak heat, or heat your gas grill to medium-high (preheated on High for 10 minutes, lid closed). Grill your steak butter-side down for about 5 minutes, until it releases easily from the grill's surface. Turn it over and cook for another 5 minutes, flipping every few minutes as you see fit, until the steak develops a nice brown crust on both sides (you will see the fat and juices bubbling through the crust as it develops—always a good sign) and reaches an internal temperature of 120°F in the middle of the steak (the readings will vary in different parts of the steak). Steak adjacent to the bone will come off rare, while the middle and edges will be more cooked—this only adds wonderful variety, showing off all the best aspects of a porterhouse. Pay extra attention to the fat cap, turning the steak on its fatty edge for a spell to cook the fat a little more.

REMOVE STEAK from the heat and very loosely wrap it in foil. Let rest for a full 15 minutes, then tidily cut the steaks from the bone. Begin with the striploin (the larger side): stand the steak upright, with the cross of the T-bone resting flat on your carving board, and cut down, riding the length of the T-bone with your knife while holding the steak with your other hand. Repeat for the tenderloin on the other side of the bone.

USING A SHARP KNIFE, cut each steak into 3/4-inch slices. Then, either on a serving platter or right on your carving board, reassemble them so each piece is back in its spot on either side of the bone, with a bit of space left between each slice. Serve immediately with a few grinds of pepper and watch the steak vanish in the blink of an eye.

CLASSIC STEAK AU POIVRE FOR TWO

Okay, this is not a classic preparation, since I've changed the recipe a little, swapping Cognac for Calvados, and adding a little grated apple to the sauce, but it tastes like a classic, I assure you. The recipe works equally well with striploin as it does with tenderloin. Creamy, a little peppery, a little smoky, with a whiff of apple—you'll declare yourself awesome after cooking and eating this, and you'll be well within your rights to do so.

SERVES 2

2 STRIPLOIN OR TENDERLOIN STEAKS
   (1 INCH THICK)
2 TEASPOONS SALT
1/2 TABLESPOON UNSALTED BUTTER, SOFTENED
4 TABLESPOONS COARSELY CRUSHED BLACK
   PEPPER (USE A BLENDER, SPICE GRINDER,
   OR MORTAR AND PESTLE)
1 SHALLOT, FINELY DICED
1/2 APPLE, PEELED, CORED, AND GRATED
1 CUP CHICKEN OR BEEF STOCK
1/4 CUP CALVADOS
1 CUP CRÈME FRAÎCHE
FRESH FLAT-LEAF PARSLEY LEAVES AND TENDER
   STEMS, CHOPPED, FOR GARNISH
ALEPPO PEPPER OR KOREAN GOCHUGARU
   PEPPER, FOR GARNISH

SEASON YOUR STEAK with salt (about 1/2 teaspoon per side). Let sit at room temperature for no longer than 30 to 40 minutes before cooking.

USING YOUR HANDS, lather butter evenly on just one side of the steak. Press a little less than 1 tablespoon black pepper onto each side of the steak, distributing it as evenly as possible.

HEAT A DRY HEAVY PAN over high heat for 5 minutes, and cook steak, butter-side down, for 2 to 3 minutes. Flip and cook the other side for another 2 to 3 minutes. Continue cooking a few more minutes, flipping as needed, until a lovely crust forms and your steak reaches an internal temperature approaching 125°F in the middle. (The steak should be pinky-red inside when checked with a small incision.) Be sure to cook the fat cap of the striploin a little by holding the fatty edge of the steak against the bottom of the pan for a minute. Remove steak from the heat (reserve pan) and very loosely wrap it in foil. Let rest while you make your pan sauce.

IN THE SAME PAN over medium heat, melt a knob of butter. Add diced shallot and grated apple, and cook until shallot softens and just begins to darken, and apple begins to disintegrate. Add stock and bring to a simmer, stirring with a wooden spoon to scrape up any brown bits at the bottom of the pan. Add Calvados and cook until the liquid has reduced by half. Stir in crème fraîche and cook, stirring briskly, until the sauce has thickened to your desired consistency. Taste, and adjust salt if necessary, then push through a fine-mesh sieve to strain out the solids (optional, but nicer).

SERVE YOUR STEAK with the creamy sauce poured overtop, sprinkled with a little chopped parsley and Aleppo pepper.

KEEP THE BONES

Once your guests have long gone and you're left with the remnants of dinner, consider keeping that rib bone or porterhouse T-bone for stock. Simply wrap the bones in foil, place in a resealable freezer bag, and freeze until you have collected enough to make a pot of stock (which for me is about 10 ribs or T-bones). When ready to make stock, place bones in a large pot and cover with 2 to 3 inches water. Add 1 large onion (skin on), halved; 2 stalks celery; 2 carrots; 6 peppercorns; 3 bay leaves; and 1 teaspoon salt. Simmer over low heat for at least 4 hours. Let cool at room temperature, then transfer to the fridge and cool until the fat solidifies. Skim off and discard fat. Discard bones and vegetables. Strain stock through a fine-mesh sieve into airtight containers. The stock can be frozen for months, or refrigerated for a week or more. It is excellent for stews and soups, sauces, and even as a warm and nourishing bone-broth drink!

TAGLIATA

This is a traditional Italian way to serve a very nice steak, generally a striploin, rib steak, or tenderloin. I've used a striploin here. Basic grilling shows off the marvellousness of the steak, with nothing more than some fresh herbs and greens, shaved Parmesan, and a good drizzle of extra-virgin olive oil. The steak should be the best you can find, and be cooked rare to medium-rare.

SERVES 1 TO 2

1 BIG STRIPLOIN STEAK (ABOUT 2 INCHES THICK)
1/2 TEASPOON SALT
1/2 TABLESPOON UNSALTED BUTTER (APPROX.), SOFTENED
1 CUP LOOSELY PACKED FRESH TENDER HERB LEAVES (SAGE, PARSLEY, THYME) OR SMALL-LEAF GREENS (ARUGULA OR LAMB'S LETTUCE)
PARMESAN CHEESE, FOR SHAVING
EXTRA-VIRGIN OLIVE OIL
FRESHLY GROUND BLACK PEPPER

SEASON YOUR STRIPLOIN with salt (about 1/4 teaspoon per side). Let sit at room temperature while you prepare your grill.

PREPARE YOUR CHARCOAL GRILL to one-third cooler than peak heat, or heat your gas grill to medium-high (preheated on High for 10 minutes, lid closed).

SLATHER BUTTER on one side of the steak. Grill, buttered-side down, for about 3 minutes, until steak can be flipped without sticking. Flip steak, then grill for 2 minutes. Continue cooking, flipping as often as you like, to develop a crust and until rare to medium-rare (approaching 120°F when tested with a meat thermometer or pinky-red inside with some red meat in the centre when checked with a small incision).

USING TONGS, gently hold the fat cap against the grill until seared; 30 seconds to 1 minute should do the trick (the cap should begin to blister, sputter, and darken a little). Remove your steak from the grill and let rest loosely wrapped in foil for at least 5 minutes.

USING A VERY SHARP KNIFE, cut your steak across its width into 1/4-inch slices. Serve on a platter or right on your carving board. Toss herbs or greens on top. Using a vegetable peeler or cheese shaver, shave Parmesan overtop. Liberally drizzle olive oil over everything. Sprinkle with salt, to taste, along with a few grinds of pepper. Just brilliant!

CULOTTE

TENDERNESS: not so tender, so slice accordingly
GRAIN: moderately coarse grain runs at
a slight angle along the length of the steak
FAT: without the fat cap, culotte is lightly speckled with fat;
the fat cap is mostly hard and generally quite thick
KEY FEATURES: coarser than a regular sirloin, but more flavourful;
the fat cap can easily be trimmed or taken completely off, or incorporated
into the cooking technique; reaches medium-rare at a slightly
lower temperature than other cuts

Behind the sirloin is a cap of muscle called culotte, or sometimes picanha if the fat cap is left intact. It can be cut into individual steaks for frying or grilling, but I like using the whole steak to take advantage of its handsome shape and straightforward slicing. The steak is a lopsided triangle, and the grain runs at a slight angle across its length, between the two farthest points of the triangle. Slicing across the grain will yield pieces with a little more chew than a typical sirloin, but I think more than manageable.

Because the steak changes shape as it cooks, I sometimes score the meat on one side to remind me which way the grain runs. If I leave the fat cap on, I always score the fat heavily, right down to the meat. Incorporating the fat as part of the steak itself is a wonderful offering. Even if your guests discard it, at least they have the option.

The muscle fibres in this steak are long, since the culotte is a single uncut muscle, and fairly strong. You will notice that it remains heavier on the grill for longer than most other cuts, and will contract, becoming thicker and rounder. This means you should be prepared to continue cooking it on a cooler part of your grill after it has developed enough crust, to bring it to

medium-rare. An instant-read meat thermometer is particularly useful here, as the culotte's size can make it tricky to gauge doneness by weight, and incision tests don't always tell the whole story. Whole culottes will reach medium-rare closer to 120°F, due in part to the way they constrict when heated quickly.

As you will see in some of the recipes in this chapter, there are ways to make the fat cap quite delectable, almost like pork crackling. The culotte, treated right, will pleasantly surprise you, and is generally about one-third of the cost of striploin. I serve it regularly to guests, who eat every last bite, asking a hundred questions about this peculiarly delicious cut of beef.

PICANHA

Picanha is a contraction of *donde se pica la aña*, which is Portuguese for "where the cow is iron-branded." In Brazil, picanha is an especially prized cut of beef and is often rotisserie cooked over a slow-burning fire or coals. When I'm gorging myself at rodizio-style (all you can eat) Brazilian churrascarias, I always leave room for picanha.

CULOTTE
(without fat cap)

PICANHA
(with fat cap)

CULOTTE WITH BLUEBERRIES AND SCAPES

GRILL

I love grilling steaks flavoured with a taste of the season. In Ontario, summertime is wild blueberry time, and blueberry stands pop up seemingly everywhere along farmsteads and at the side of highways in cottage country. Blueberry season happens to coincide nicely with the season for scapes, which are cut from garlic stalks to encourage the bulbs to grow larger and are sold at farmers' markets. Errant garlic shows up every year in my back garden from discarded cloves left in my compost all winter, so I always find myself with an embarrassment of scapes, some of which I pickle, and some of which I cook up into this bright and woodsy, marvellously beefy steak.

1 BUNCH OF GARLIC SCAPES (5 OR 6 STALKS), DIVIDED, HALF FINELY DICED (SEE TIPS)
1 CUP FRESH BLUEBERRIES (WILD OR REGULAR)
3 OR 4 DRIED JUNIPER BERRIES OR 1 SPRIG FRESH ROSEMARY, LEAVES CHOPPED AND STALK LEFT WHOLE
2 TABLESPOONS EXTRA-VIRGIN OLIVE OIL
PINCH OF SALT (PREFERABLY GREY SEA SALT OR ROCK SALT)
1 CULOTTE STEAK (2 POUNDS OR MORE)
FRESHLY GROUND BLACK PEPPER

SERVES 4 TO 6

USING A MORTAR AND PESTLE, crush together diced scapes, blueberries, juniper berries (or rosemary, including the stalk, removing it and discarding it when you're done), olive oil, and a big pinch of salt. The result should be a rather fragrant, somewhat piney, dark purple paste.

USING A SHARP KNIFE, score the steak at 1/4-inch intervals. Rub the blueberry scape paste into your culotte and let sit at room temperature for 30 minutes to 1 hour, preferably longer (you can do this a day ahead, keeping it refrigerated until you're ready).

MEANWHILE, in a pot of boiling salted water, parboil reserved whole scapes for 90 seconds, until they soften slightly but are still bright green (this is so they are tender enough to eat after they are grilled).

PREPARE YOUR CHARCOAL GRILL to one-third cooler than peak heat, or heat your gas grill to medium-high (preheated on High for 10 minutes, lid closed).

PLACE YOUR CULOTTE on the grill and cook until the steak reaches an internal temperature approaching 120°F in the middle (earlier than most cuts, but trust me—it will even out to medium-rare once it has rested). When your steak is done, remove it from the grill and let rest loosely wrapped in foil for 10 minutes while you grill your scapes. Remove the scapes when nicely browned.

USING A SHARP KNIFE, cut the steak across the grain into 1/4-inch slices. Serve on a platter or your carving board with the grilled scapes, along with the juices from the foil. Season with salt and pepper, to taste.

TIPS: If you don't have any scapes on hand, you can substitute 1 clove garlic, finely grated, and 3 scallions (1 sliced for the marinade, and 2 whole for grilling—no need to parboil). As an alternative to grilling the steak, you can reverse-sear it on your stovetop. Heat a dry heavy pan over high heat, and sear steak for 2 minutes per side. (See page 33 for how to reverse-sear.)

CLEMENTINE PICANHA

The smell of orange peel will fill your kitchen as the culotte slowly makes its way to just the right temperature, awaiting its final sear. I've left the fat cap on, scoring it so that it is crosshatched just as you might a duck breast. Once sliced, the culotte is a complete bite: savoury meat, crackling-style fat, and a fabulous marmalade taste that makes this recipe truly out of the ordinary.

SERVES 4 TO 6

1 CULOTTE STEAK (2 POUNDS OR MORE),
   FAT CAP ON (PICANHA-STYLE)
1 TEASPOON SALT
2 CLEMENTINE ORANGES, FOR ZESTING
   AND JUICING
2 CLOVES GARLIC (1 FINELY GRATED,
   THE OTHER THINLY SLICED)
1 TABLESPOON COINTREAU
FRESHLY GROUND BLACK PEPPER

LINE THE BOTTOM RACK of your oven with enough foil to catch any drippings. Preheat your oven to 225°F.

IF THE FAT CAP on your culotte is particularly hefty, trim it to a thickness of about 1/4 inch using a sharp knife. Then score the fat cap, first across and then lengthwise, so you end up with 1/4-inch-square crosshatching.

RUB THE PREPARED CULOTTE with salt (about 1/2 teaspoon per side). Squeeze the juice from 1/2 of the clementine over the crosshatched fat cap. Cut the remaining 1/2 clementine into thin slices and insert into several of the scored slits. Do the same with the sliced garlic. Carefully rub some minced garlic on the fat cap and sides of the steak. Zest the remaining clementine and sprinkle over the fat cap.

PLACE STEAK on a wire rack and transfer to the upper rack of your preheated oven. Cook for 30 minutes per pound or until the steak reaches an internal temperature approaching 115°F in the middle (or an average of about 118°F with several checks in different areas of the steak).

ON YOUR STOVETOP over high heat, heat a dry, heavy pan until very hot. Sear your culotte on both sides, starting with the fat-side down (it will sputter and render fat into the pan, which is good). Take extra care when you sear the fat side so it doesn't get too dark; there should be both black and dark brown parts. When the steak reaches an internal temperature approaching 120°F in the middle (which is earlier than most cuts; culotte is special that way), remove it from the heat (reserve the pan) and let rest loosely wrapped in foil for at least 10 minutes.

IN THE SAME PAN, over medium heat, add the juice of the remaining clementine and a splash of Cointreau. Cook, stirring up any browned bits with a wooden spoon, until the liquid (including the rendered fat) thickens to a sauce. Stir in the juices from the foil and let reduce for another minute, until you reach your desired consistency.

USING A SHARP KNIFE, slice the steak across the grain. Serve with some of the sauce drizzled overtop, and the rest in a small bowl for passing. Season with ground pepper.

CULOTTE WITH FIGGY MARMITE JUNIPER GLAZE

REVERSE-SEAR

Dried juniper berries are best here, but you can use smashed rosemary to approximate the juniper flavour. The glaze will be rich and salty, with the perfume of peppery pine. I like to serve any leftover glaze as a sauce, with aged cheddar on toast, and pan-fried endive.

SERVES 4 TO 6

1 CULOTTE STEAK (ABOUT 2 POUNDS), CAP REMOVED

1 TABLESPOON MARMITE, DIVIDED

DUCK FAT OR UNSALTED BUTTER OR LARD OR TALLOW

2 TABLESPOONS UNSALTED BUTTER, DIVIDED

8 DRIED JUNIPER BERRIES, SMASHED WITH A MORTAR AND PESTLE

1 FRESH FIG

1 CUP DRY RED WINE

AS MUCH ENDIVE AS YOU LIKE, HALVED LENGTHWISE

1 OR MORE SHALLOTS, QUARTERED BUT ROOT END LEFT INTACT TO HOLD LAYERS TOGETHER

LINE THE BOTTOM RACK of your oven with enough foil to catch any drippings. Preheat oven to 225°F.

THIS STEP IS OPTIONAL, but it helps you remember which way the grain runs after cooking has changed the steak's shape and hidden the granularity on its surface: Using a sharp knife, lightly score your culotte across its length, between the two furthest corners of its triangular shape (which is the same direction as the grain).

USING YOUR HANDS, spread a thin coating of Marmite all over the steak. Place the steak on a wire rack in preheated oven and cook for 30 minutes per pound, turning once halfway through to dry both sides evenly. Remove from oven when the steak reaches an internal temperature approaching 115°F in the middle, or an average of 118°F when tested in different parts.

USING YOUR HANDS or a basting brush, coat one side of the steak with a big dab of duck fat. In a heavy pan over high heat, sear steak on both sides, starting fat-side down. When the steak reaches an internal temperature approaching 120°F (which is cooler than the other cuts since the culotte reaches medium-rare faster) and your crust looks fabulously dark and handsome, remove it from the heat (reserve the pan). (If the steak starts to

look like it's going to get too dark before you are able to bring it to temperature, reduce the heat to medium.) Let steak rest loosely wrapped in foil for at least 10 minutes while you prepare the sauce and endive.

IN THE RESERVED PAN, combine 1 tablespoon butter, smashed juniper berries, and 1/2 teaspoon Marmite and heat until the butter starts to bubble. Add fig and, using a wooden spoon, squash it in the pan. Pour in red wine and cook, stirring with a wooden spoon to pick up any brown bits at the bottom of the pan, until the mixture thickens to a syrupy glaze and is reduced by half. Pour in the juices from the foil wrapped around your steak and stir well. Transfer sauce to a small bowl and set aside (reserve pan).

TO THE SAME PAN over medium-high heat, melt 1 tablespoon butter. Fry endive and shallots until softened and darkened, about 2 minutes. Remove from heat and set aside.

USING A VERY SHARP KNIFE, cut your culotte into 1/4-inch slices across the grain and transfer to a serving platter or serve on your carving board. Drizzle glaze overtop and scatter with endive halves and shallot wedges. Serve with a little bowl of the delicious figgy Marmite glaze on the side.

CHERRY-GRILLED PICANHA

GRILL

Early summer is cherry season, and there is nothing like marrying up the flavours of a big, meaty steak with the deep, dark taste of cherries, especially when the cherries are cooked a little. This recipe requires a little grill management because of the substantial fat cap on the steak, but other than that, it's dead simple, lots of fun, and looks and tastes spectacular.

SERVES 4 TO 6

1 CULOTTE STEAK (ABOUT 3 POUNDS), FAT CAP ON (PICANHA-STYLE)

1 TEASPOON SALT

1 POUND CHERRIES (ENOUGH TO FILL A HEAPING CEREAL BOWL), 8 PITTED AND SQUASHED

1 TEASPOON LIQUID HONEY

USING A SHARP BONING KNIFE or chef's knife, trim any excess from your culotte's fat cap to 1/4 inch thick. Score the fat cap in both directions, right down to the meat, to create a crosshatch pattern. Sprinkle salt liberally all over the steak, rubbing it into the crevices of the fat cap. Rub the squashed cherries and honey all over the steak, especially in the fat cap. Let sit at room temperature while you prepare your grill.

PREPARE YOUR CHARCOAL GRILL to one-third cooler than peak heat, or heat your gas grill to medium-high (preheated on High for 10 minutes, lid closed). For charcoal grills, gather the hot coals to one side of the grill bowl. For gas grills, turn one side of the grill completely off; if you like, place a cake pan with a little water in the bottom on the unlit side, under the grill, to catch any fat drippings.

GRILL YOUR CULOTTE until medium-rare (approaching 120°F when checked with a meat thermometer, or pinky-red inside when tested with a small incision), turning as necessary. The crosshatched fat will blacken and shrink into chewy, sticky nodes of taffy-like goodness. It will also cause some fairly major flare-ups when the culotte is fat-side down on the grill. Watch for this, and simply move the steak to the unfired half of the grill and close the lid—you can cook fat-side down as you need to, roasting the steak with ambient heat. Let steak rest loosely wrapped in foil for at least 10 minutes while you grill the remaining cherries.

PLACE WHOLE CHERRIES (with pits) directly on the grill, and cook until softened and blistered, and they begin to expel a little juice.

USING A VERY SHARP KNIFE, cut your steak into 1/4-inch slices across the grain and transfer to a serving platter or serve on your carving board. Scatter grilled cherries overtop. Drizzle some of the juices from the foil over the steak, and serve the rest in a small bowl on the side.

TIPS: Charcoal grills will get hotter inside for a while, then start to cool as the coals suffocate. Gas grills don't suffer from this. In both cases, you will want to raise the hood when you grill the lean side of the culotte, to manage the cooking properly and allow the other side to cool somewhat between turns. For a steak this big—culottes are thick and get thicker as they ball up while cooking—longer grilling time works well. Use one side of your grill for direct grilling, and the other side for ambient-heat cooking (with the lid closed) and fat-cap management.

CHERRY WOOD SMOKE

Closing your grill hood while cooking presents a terrific opportunity to add more smoky flavour to your food. Try throwing some cherry wood trimmings or pellets (soaked first) directly on the hot coals. For gas grills, put the soaked wood in a pouch of aluminum foil, puncture it a few times to let out some smoke, and place on the burner or heating plate. You only need a few minutes of this smoke under the grill hood to impart real cherry wood flavour to your meat.

SKIRT

TENDERNESS: Controversial. A lot of people insist it's tough, but if sliced
thinly I think it's easy to chew whether cut across the grain or not.
GRAIN: wide, loose grain runs across the width
FAT: nicely fatted, evenly distributed
KEY FEATURES: Richly flavourful, with a delightful texture.
A few of my butcher friends describe it as "buttery" tasting. I think they're right.

When I can stop dreaming of prime rib steak long enough, I really do think that skirt steak is my next favourite. It is very well fatted between its large, loose fibres, cooks easily and quickly, and is forgiving a little past medium-rare. Thin slices of less than 1/4 inch will yield a bite that is sufficiently tender for most steak eaters. The skirt steak is a great example of a cut that is not technically tender in terms of shear, but feels tender enough because of its texture and consistency, not unlike bavette.

The fat in skirt steak is soft and melts quickly. It seems particularly tasty, too, and there is hardly a need to oil a pan or your steak as you place it on the grill (but I give one side a very thin coat, just in case).

There are two types of skirt steaks: the inside skirt and the outside skirt. There is some confusion between the two, even among steak enthusiasts. The first thing to remember is that, for the purposes of grilling steak, there really isn't that much difference—both are skirts, after all. But let's break it down.

The outside skirt is responsible for moving the diaphragm in the live animal, and is just a little more tender. It is attached to the rib cage, running around the outside of the abdominal wall (thus "outside" skirt). It is thinner than an inside skirt from the same animal, which is why it is sometimes called a thin skirt. It is the original *fajita*, which means "little belt" in Spanish,

because that's what it reminded people of, winding as a belt around the thoracic cavity. It is occasionally sold with its membrane still attached (this is the diaphragm itself). For all the recipes in this book, the membrane needs to be removed before cooking. Let your butcher do that for you.

The inside skirt, responsible for compressing the abdomen, is a little less tender and slightly thicker than an outside skirt from the same animal, with a somewhat wider grain. Being attached to the flank steak, it is sometimes included as part of the flank, as it is in Argentina, making for the very large matambre steak, big enough to stuff and roll. (If that has raised an eyebrow, see the matambre recipe on page 132.)

Both skirts are about 15 inches or more in length, and just 1/2 inch or more thick. The best way to max out the tenderness if you're not serving it as a single, unsliced portion, is to grill it whole, cut it into 5-inch pieces, and then slice those pieces across the grain. The best way to cook it is quickly, with a lot of heat, to get a nice colour and to flavour your crust without overcooking the meat.

If you don't feel like reading a recipe, know that you can simply cook a skirt steak over a hot grill or in a hot pan for 5 to 7 minutes and be pretty happy with it.

STEAK TACOS

FRY

The buttery taste and loose texture of skirt steak makes it perfect for tacos. Essential advice: cut the skirt thinly across the grain, and use real (soft) corn tortillas. Toppings are up to you, but the ones I've listed here have worked their combined magic for me over the years (the crème fraîche almost always making an appearance). If you don't care to make the chili rub, you can just use regular store-bought chili powder.

MAKES 6 TACOS

1 POUND SKIRT STEAK
FAT, FOR COOKING (DUCK FAT, GOOSE FAT, LARD, NICE BACON FAT, SUET, TALLOW, SCHMALTZ), OR COOKING OIL
6 SOFT CORN TORTILLAS (WRAPPED IN FOIL AND WARMED IN THE OVEN OR TOASTER OVEN)

CHILI RUB
2 TABLESPOONS GROUND DRIED ANCHO CHILIES (OR YOUR FAVOURITE MILD CHILIES)
1 TEASPOON GROUND CORIANDER
1 TEASPOON GROUND CUMIN
1/4 TEASPOON GROUND NUTMEG
1/4 TEASPOON GROUND CINNAMON
PINCH OF SALT

TOPPINGS (1 CUP EACH)
REFRIED BEANS, PREFERABLY HOMEMADE (SEE PAGE 197)
LETTUCE, SHREDDED OR JULIENNED
AVOCADO, SLICED
ONION, DICED
RADISH, DICED
QUESO FRESCO OR FETA CHEESE
CRÈME FRAÎCHE
YOUR FAVOURITE HOT SAUCE

IN A BOWL, combine all of the chili rub ingredients.

DUST BOTH SIDES of your steak with the chili rub until well coated. Store any leftover chili rub in an airtight container for your next taco meal.

IN A CAST-IRON, heavy stainless-steel, or non-stick pan (with a heavy heat-cookie bottom) over medium-high, heat the fat. Fry your steak until it develops a nice crust and reaches medium-rare (125°F) or medium (135°F) when tested with a meat thermometer (when checked with a small incision for medium-rare, it should appear pinky-red with some red meat in the middle and flowing juices), flipping as often as you like, 6 to 7 minutes total. Let rest loosely wrapped in foil for 5 to 10 minutes while you prepare the rest of your ingredients.

ARRANGE YOUR TOPPINGS of choice in small bowls, alongside the tortillas and a bottle of your favourite hot sauce.

ON A CARVING BOARD, cut the skirt steak into thin slices, across the grain. Transfer slices to a bowl along with the juice from the carving board and foil.

LOAD UP your tacos and enjoy!

CHARCOAL-SEARED SKIRT WITH CHIMICHURRI

A really fun way to cook a skirt steak to perfection and with a terrific crust is to lay it directly on the hot charcoal. It may sound crazy to the uninitiated, but it is a blast, and your friends will think you are a maverick. Hot coals aren't actually dirty, so simply fan the ash from the coals before grilling. The taste of direct charcoal cooking is like nothing else.

Skirt steak goes incredibly well with tangy, fresh raw sauces like chimichurri, which is a traditional sauce in Mexico, Argentina, and other regions across Latin America. Chimichurri recipes change from region to region, and even from neighbourhood to neighbourhood, but they all have this in common: they are brothy and acidic, and generally include a big helping of either fresh parsley or fresh cilantro. The recipe I've included here has worked really well for me over the years. I'm actually worried that once you try skirt steak and chimichurri together, you will close this book and call it a day. It's that good.

1 SKIRT STEAK (ABOUT 2 POUNDS)
1/2 TEASPOON SALT
FRESHLY GROUND BLACK PEPPER
1 1/2 TABLESPOONS EXTRA-VIRGIN OLIVE OIL, DIVIDED
1 MEDIUM RIPE TOMATO, COARSELY GRATED ON THE LARGE HOLES OF A BOX GRATER, WITH JUICE
1 SHALLOT, FINELY DICED
1 CLOVE GARLIC, MINCED
1/2 BUNCH OF FRESH CILANTRO, LEAVES ROUGHLY CHOPPED AND TENDER STEMS VERY FINELY CHOPPED (ABOUT 1 CUP)
JUICE OF 1/2 LIME
1/2 TABLESPOON SWEET VINEGAR (LIKE RICE VINEGAR OR WHITE BALSAMIC)
1/2 TEASPOON HOT PEPPER FLAKES

SERVES 4

SEASON BOTH SIDES of your skirt steak with 1/4 teaspoon salt and pepper to taste. Rub a really thin coating of olive oil on the less fatty side. Let sit at room temperature while you prepare your chimichurri and grill.

IN A BOWL, combine grated tomato and its juice, shallot, garlic, cilantro, 1 tablespoon olive oil, lime juice, vinegar, hot pepper flakes, and salt to taste. Taste and adjust the oil and vinegar as desired, but the mixture should be quite tangy. Set aside to let the flavours meld.

PREPARE HARDWOOD CHARCOAL for cooking, and wait until the coals have whitened completely and your fire is just off peak heat (about 5 extra minutes). With a piece of cardboard (or an old-fashioned hand fan), fan the coals to blow off the ash. Three or four gusts should do it. You will never get the surface of the coals perfectly clean, and that doesn't matter.

GENTLY LAY THE SKIRT STEAK on the hot, clean coals, oil-side down. Skirt steaks are long, so you will need to either cut it in half or lay it down loosely,

so the whole steak is in contact with just the coals and not the side of your coal kettle. Cook for 2 to 3 minutes, until the edges start to darken a little. Then, using long cooking tongs, turn the steak over and cook the other side for another 2 to 3 minutes. Transfer the steak to a carving board, and test it for doneness by making a small incision: juices should flow from a medium-rare (pinky-red) centre; if they don't, put the steak back on the coals for another minute or so until they do. Let steak rest loosely wrapped in foil for 5 minutes (skirt steaks don't need long to rest).

USING A SHARP KNIFE, cut your steak into 1/4-inch slices. If you want to slice across the grain, cut the steak in half—or into 3 or 4 pieces, depending how long you want your slices—and then rotate each piece so the grain is perpendicular to your knife. Slice the steak on an angle from top to bottom, for a nice shape and more meat per slice.

SERVE YOUR STEAK with chimichurri on the side.

TORCHA SAUCE

A few summers ago, during one of my visits to the farmers' market at Wychwood Barns in Toronto, [t]ook some advice from a cacao dealer, whose chocolate I would buy nearly every week. He travelled to Mexico for his cacao beans, and heard this recipe from one of the farmers he routinely did business with[.] The sauce is zesty and firey, and great with steak (and nachos!).

[1] OR 2 SMALL DRIED HOT CHILIES
   (LIKE ÁRBOL CHILIES)
[2] CLOVES GARLIC
[1]0 CHERRY OR GRAPE TOMATOES
[1] LIME, HALVED
[1] TABLESPOON EXTRA-VIRGIN OLIVE OIL
[1]/4 CUP CILANTRO OR FLAT-LEAF PARSLEY
[P]INCH OF SALT

[M]AKES ENOUGH FOR 4 TO 6 STEAK EATERS

[H]EAT A DRY cast-iron pan over medium-high heat. [A]dd dried chilies (if you like, break open and discard [s]eeds to reduce their pepper), and cook until they blis-[t]er and char a little. Grind them in a mortar and pestle, [a]nd set aside.

[A]DD GARLIC to the hot pan, and cook until it [b]lackens a little. Transfer to the mortar and pestle with [c]hilies, grind until they fall apart, and set aside.

ADD TOMATOES to the hot pan, and sauté until they blister and char a little. Transfer to the mortar and pestle.

FINALLY, COOK halved lime, cut-side down, in the hot pan for a minute or two, until its juice cooks a little and the cut side caramelizes. Remove pan from the heat and set aside.

TO THE MORTAR and pestle, add olive oil, cilantro juice of cooked lime, and salt. Pulverize everything together until the sauce resembles a somewhat brothy, chunky salsa.

SERVE IMMEDIATELY or cover and refrigerate for several days.

TIP: You can make this on the grill, too. Use skewers for the garlic cloves so they don't fall through the grating.

QUICK AND DIRTY SEVEN-THIRTY SKIRT (A MEAL FOR ONE)

It's 7:30 p.m., and you just got home from work. Do you know where your dinner is? If not, don't worry. This recipe (a whole meal) will have you in and out of the kitchen faster than you can order a pizza—and you get to have a steak.

SERVES 1

1 SINGLE SERVING-SIZE SKIRT STEAK (6 OUNCES)
CHILI POWDER (OR SEE RECIPE ON PAGE 123)
2 TABLESPOONS UNSALTED BUTTER, DIVIDED
OLIVE OIL, FOR FRYING
1 MEDIUM ONION, DICED
1 CUP WATER
1/2 CUP SHORT- OR LONG-GRAIN BROWN RICE
1 LARGE EGG
1/2 CAN (7 TO 8 FL. OZ) PINTO BEANS, BLACK
    BEANS, OR RED BEANS, RINSED AND DRAINED
MICROGREENS, FOR SERVING
1 LEMON WEDGE
SALT AND PEPPER

SPRINKLE chili spice all over your skirt steak and pat it in so it sticks (enough to coat but not so much that it cakes).

IN A FRYING PAN over medium heat, melt 1 tablespoon butter with a splash of olive oil. Add onion and cook until golden brown. Transfer to a bowl and set aside, reserving pan.

IN A SAUCEPAN, combine water, rice, and egg (shell on). Cover, and bring to a boil. Once boiling, reduce the heat and simmer for 5 minutes. Remove the nearly hard-boiled egg and set aside. Cover pan and simmer for another 10 minutes (for a total of about 20 minutes). Fold in beans, cover, and cook until the rice just starts to stick to the bottom of the pot, about 5 minutes longer (the rice should be soft, with just a little bit of extra stiffness left in the centre). Fold in browned onions with remaining 1 tablespoon butter, then set pot aside.

HEAT RESERVED FRYING PAN over high heat until you can feel heat emanating when you hold your hand 2 inches above the pan's cooking surface, about 4 minutes. Add your seasoned skirt steak and cook, flipping as you see fit, until both sides develop a rather

dark crust, about 5 minutes total. Check your steak for doneness with a small incision: juices should flow from a medium-rare (pinky-red) centre. If they don't, cook steak for another minute or two until they do. Let steak rest loosely wrapped in foil for 5 minutes (skirts don't need much resting time).

MEANWHILE, peel the hard-boiled egg (the yolk's centre should still be a tiny bit runny) and cut it in half lengthwise. Set aside.

PLACE MICROGREENS in a bowl, splash with a little lemon juice and olive oil, and season with salt and pepper.

SERVE THE SKIRT whole or cut into 1/4-inch slices (across the grain if you like, and on a bias to get more steak surface per slice), with the dirty rice and beans, the boiled egg, and your dressed microgreens alongside.

TIP: This recipe works equally well grilling the skirt steak on a hot grill. Just make the rice ahead of time.

PAN-FRIED SKIRT
WITH CAPERS, BLISTERED CHERRY TOMATOES, AND SMASH-FRIED POTATOES

There is a way to do this on the grill, skewering the tomatoes instead of quick-frying them, and grilling the potato with a brush of butter, but I do like the way the pan treats the smashed potato, and the capers and lemon cooked with the tomatoes gives this element a tangy boost, tying the whole dish together. I make this dish a lot when I want to grill but can't because it's raining (or freezing). Best rainy night ever.

EACH STEAK SERVES 1

AS MANY SKIRT STEAKS AS YOU LIKE (ABOUT 6 OUNCES EACH)

PER STEAK PORTION
SALT AND PEPPER
1 MEDIUM POTATO
2 TABLESPOONS FAT OF YOUR CHOICE, DIVIDED
1 SHALLOT, DICED
LEMON SLICES, CUT INTO 5 OR 6 CAPER-SIZED TRIANGLES
CAPERS, EXCESS BRINE GENTLY SQUEEZED OUT
4 CHERRY TOMATOES
CRÈME FRAÎCHE OR SOUR CREAM
FRESH FLAT-LEAF PARSLEY, FOR GARNISH

SEASON YOUR SKIRT STEAKS with a dusting of salt on both sides, and let sit at room temperature while you cook the potatoes.

FILL A SAUCEPAN with water and boil whole potatoes until tender, about 25 minutes (or microwave on High for 5 minutes per potato). Drain and set aside.

HEAT A HEAVY FRYING PAN over high heat until you can feel heat emanating when you hold your hand 2 inches above the pan's cooking surface, about 4 minutes. Melt 1 tablespoon of fat, and cook your seasoned skirt steak until medium-rare, flipping as needed. Check your steak for doneness with a small incision: juices should flow from a medium-rare (pinky-red) centre. If they don't, cook steak for another minute or two until they do (it won't be as dark or as evenly crusted as you might be able to get a thicker steak, but that's okay). Let steak rest loosely wrapped in foil for 5 minutes (skirts don't need much resting time) while you finish the dish (reserve the pan).

USING THE PALM of your hand, squash the cooked potatoes into rough pancakes (be gentle: you don't want them to fall apart). Place reserved pan over medium-high heat and fry squashed potatoes, flipping as needed, until browned and getting crispy at the edges, about 4 minutes. Transfer to individual serving plates and set aside.

IN THE SAME PAN, still over medium-high heat, melt remaining 1 tablespoon of fat. Add shallot, lemon triangles, and capers and cook for 1 minute, stirring occasionally. Add tomatoes and cook for about 1 minute, until the tomatoes start to blister and give up their juices (but still maintain their structure) and the shallot is softened and slightly browned. Remove from heat.

TO SERVE, top each smashed potato with 1 tablespoon crème fraîche, then place individual skirt steak portions on top (either whole or cut across the grain, on a bias, into 1/4-inch slices, to maximize the surface area of the slice). Tumble blistered cherry tomatoes, shallot, and capers on top of this, followed by another dollop of crème fraîche. Sprinkle with chopped parsley and a few grinds of pepper, and serve.

FLANK

TENDERNESS: moderately tender if sliced across the grain; a bit of a chew if not
GRAIN: medium to coarse, well-defined grain runs along the length
FAT: moderately fatted, evenly distributed
KEY FEATURES: The perfect grilling steak for a crowd. The direction of the grain makes it a cinch to slice for tenderness. It holds its moisture well up to medium-rare.

When I was a teenager, I used to work for a big German man named Dieter Scheffler at Toronto's St. Lawrence Market. I would get there every Saturday at 5:00 a.m. and start yelling out prices and packing up orders of fresh wieners, bratwurst, house-smoked bacon, and deli meats, while Herr Scheffler chatted with the crowd and worked the slicer. Sometimes he would show people his right thumb, which he had sliced off past the second knuckle years earlier.

As the market began to close for the day, I would scan other vendors' stalls to see what was left after the vanishing crowd had bought their preference. I took home a lot of turnips, a lot of odd-shaped carrots, and more often than not, a flank steak. These last things to go were always on sale, and that fit my budget. If I could imagine why perfect carrots sold before those shaped like a mandrake, I could never understand why flank steak wasn't sold first off the block. Cooked right, and sliced right, it is exactly what one might crave. Flank became my go-to steak in those formative years, whether it was on sale or not.

Flank steak is cut from the bottom of the cow, near the belly, and is part of the abdomen muscle group. It is about the size and shape of a flatbread, at 12 to 15 inches long, 7 to 9 inches across, and about an inch thick, sometimes tapering a little at either end. It does a fair amount of work for the live animal, so it's not all that tender unless it is cooked close to medium-rare and sliced across the grain. Luckily, that's really easy with the flank steak. The grain is not as loose as skirt or bavette, but it is easy enough to distinguish, and runs right along its length. The meat is firm, and is as compliant as a cucumber to a sharp knife, which glides through easily without moving it around. This means you can cut the steak at a severe bias to get thin, broad, handsome slices easily. I like to cut the flank in half down its length before grilling it, for long steaks that slice up tidily and look great on the plate.

Flank steak doesn't appreciate overcooking, even to medium, and I don't think its potential is realized fully if it's cooked just to rare. So you want to get it right on medium-rare, or just to either side of it. Another bit of luck: it is really easy to check flank for doneness with a small incision. The doneness of the middle is plain to see because the grain is relatively dense and the steak is thin, giving you a very good idea of what's happening with one quick look inside. Instant-read thermometers can work, too, but sometimes the flank is thin enough that it's hard to know if your reading is from the middle of the steak or closer to the outer surface.

Even with these caveats, if I had to cook a whole lot of steak for someone's wedding, it would be flank. Once you get used to its character, it will come off the grill with amazing consistency and is a universal crowd pleaser. Its rustic texture seems to ask for a little spice, and it does well with a dry rub, which will help the crust develop in time for the medium-rare middle.

130

BRAD JOLLY'S FLANK MATAMBRE

Matambre, as far as I can tell, is an Argentine mash-up of "kill" (*matar*) and "hunger" (*hambre*), and it is sumptuous and substantial enough to do exactly that. It also refers to the Argentine cut of beef, like a flank but not exactly. In any case, I use a flank here because it's easy to find—besides, that's what my friend Brad used when he cooked it up on a surprise drop-in at my place. Like me, Brad is fond of big, deep flavours, and his matambre recipe does not disappoint. Serve with creamy polenta or mashed potatoes, and a little of the deep-red braising broth ladled on top. Your dinner guests will leave immensely sated and eternally grateful. I know I was that night my epicurean friend dropped by.

SERVES 6

1 TABLESPOON NICE FRYING FAT (GOOSE FAT, DUCK FAT, LARD, TALLOW, OR SCHMALTZ)

1 EACH LEEK, ONION, AND SHALLOT, ROUGHLY CHOPPED

5 EACH PITTED GREEN AND KALAMATA OLIVES

8 SUNDRIED TOMATO HALVES, HALF OF THEM FINELY CHOPPED

6 ANCHOVY FILLETS, CHOPPED

4 CLOVES GARLIC, FINELY CHOPPED

1 TABLESPOON DRIED ALEPPO OR GOCHUGARU PEPPER

2 OUNCES FRESHLY GRATED PARMESAN CHEESE (ABOUT 1/2 CUP)

1/4 CUP CHOPPED FRESH FLAT-LEAF PARSLEY

1 FLANK STEAK (ABOUT 2 POUNDS), BUTTERFLIED

4 STRIPS BACON

1/2 CUP ROASTED RED PEPPERS, CUT INTO STRIPS

2 CUPS TOMATO PASSATA

2 CUPS DRY VERMOUTH

2 CUPS BEEF OR CHICKEN STOCK

4 BAY LEAVES

PREHEAT your oven to 275°F.

IN A LARGE FRYING PAN, heat fat of choice. Sauté leek, onion, shallot, olives, sundried tomatoes, anchovies, garlic, and Aleppo pepper until the onions have softened, about 5 minutes. Stir in Parmesan and parsley, and then remove pan from the heat and set aside.

PLACE FLANK STEAK on a clean work surface. Arrange a single layer of bacon and red pepper strips in flat rows across the steak. Top with half of leek mixture, gently spreading it as evenly as you can (transfer remaining mixture to a bowl and set aside, and reserve pan). Starting at one short end, carefully roll up steak like a sleeping bag. Tie each end quite tightly with butcher's string, closing it like a sausage. Secure the remaining parts with four or five lengths of string to help it maintain its shape.

ADD A LITTLE more butter to the frying pan you used to sauté the filling, and brown the rolled-up flank on medium-high heat until a nice crust develops.

IN A LARGE POT or roasting pan, combine passata, vermouth, stock, bay leaves, and the remaining filling mixture. Add prepared flank and roast, covered, for 3 hours. Your matambre will be very tender but will still hold its shape without falling apart when you lift it.

CAREFULLY SLICE and serve with a spoonful of braising liquid.

GARLIC-MISO FLANK

GRILL

I love the fermented, salty flavours of Japanese savoury dishes. On steak, this skyrockets the flavour into the umamisphere, making every bite a sultry sensation. On flank steak, the coating also lets you cook the steak to rare or medium-rare so you can be assured of a delightfully dark and sumptuous crust, which will greatly please the Steak Gods, not to mention your dinner guests.

SERVES 4 TO 6

5 TABLESPOONS DARK MISO

3 TABLESPOONS SAKE (OR DRY VERMOUTH, BUT SAKE IS BETTER)

2 TABLESPOONS LIQUID HONEY

1 TABLESPOON GROUND DRIED GOCHUGARU OR ALEPPO PEPPER

1/2 TABLESPOON COCONUT OIL (OR ANOTHER OIL, BUT COCONUT WORKS BETTER HERE)

4 CLOVES GARLIC, FINELY GRATED

1 WHOLE FLANK STEAK (ABOUT 2 POUNDS)

IN A BOWL, combine miso, sake, honey, gochugaru, coconut oil, and garlic until you have an even paste. Using your hands, rub it evenly all over your flank steak. Starting at a short end, roll the steak up like a sleeping bag. Set aside at room temperature for 30 minutes while you prepare your grill.

PREPARE YOUR CHARCOAL GRILL to one-third cooler than peak heat, or heat your gas grill to medium-high (preheated on High for 10 minutes, lid closed).

USING A SHARP KNIFE, cut rolled-up steak in half right down the middle across its width, to get two narrower steaks. If the miso marinade thickly coats the flank steak, scrape some off (the steak should be thoroughly coated but not excessively goopy).

GRILL YOUR STEAK until it reaches an internal temperature of 110°F in the meaty middle. (This will get you to a perfect rare. If you want it medium-rare, which is completely acceptable, cook until the internal temperature is 120°F. In either case, your crust should be dark and sticky.) Very loosely wrap steak in foil and set aside for 5 to 10 minutes. You may want to check for doneness with a small incision in this case, to get a better idea: the steak should be pinky-red inside, with some running juices and some rare meat in the very middle.

USING A SHARP KNIFE, cut your grilled steak across its width (across the grain) on a bias (really just for shape) into 1/4-inch slices. Pour juices from the foil and carving board into a ramekin or small cup, and serve alongside, for pouring or dipping.

COOKING WITH COCONUT OIL

Coconut oil is also a wonderful cooking oil, and unlike almost every other plant-based oil, is naturally saturated (like animal fats it too remains stable when heated, avoiding the health issues associated with free radicals in food). Like lard or duck fat, coconut oil is solid at or under room temperature. It's not altogether taste-neutral, though, so your food may smack just a little of coconut when you cook with it. Not always a bad thing!

BAVETTE

TENDERNESS: moderately tender if sliced across the grain; a bit of a chew if not

GRAIN: wide, loose grain runs across the width

FAT: moderately fatted, evenly distributed

KEY FEATURES: richly flavourful, with a splendid texture; big steak when whole, with varying thicknesses to work with; engorged, and holds its moisture well

Bavette was the first non-loin, non-rib steak I ever tried. It was served to me at Toronto's Le Select Bistro, many years ago, with their classic matchstick frites. They cut the portion from the thickest part of the steak, so at the time I had no idea of its shape. Whole, the bavette looks like a massively overgrown skirt steak (the one in the photo opposite is cut in half), and some folks occasionally confuse the two. Bavette is also sometimes called sirloin flap meat, because it comes from the end of the sirloin as the loin transitions into the middle part of the cow, near the flank. Whole bavette steaks are 15 to 20 inches long, and up to 2 inches thick in the middle, tapering off considerably at either end, weighing 3 to 5 pounds—really great to serve to a crowd.

When butcher shops began to offer bavette regularly, I bought some nearly every weekend for an entire summer. It's marvellous grilled, and you can grill it hot, to get a nice crust, even if you marinate it. *Bavette* is a French word, and they are so enamoured with this steak that they parse it into three distinct bavette cuts. The Argentines are also very fond of it. They call it *vacio*,

and grill it asado-style over live fire. I generally cook it whole and happily end up with leftovers if I'm alone, or reliably with not a scrap left if I'm cooking for a group. Because bavette is a lot thicker in its middle than at its ends, you can't avoid having the steak cooked to different doneness across its length. That's okay, because some of your crowd might secretly prefer the well-done ends over the medium-rare middle. If you're mean, you can watch for this and call them out. Truth be told, those crispy bits at the ends are really nice.

You can pan-fry bavette, but, like hanger steak, it tends to perform better on a hot grill. The thinnest sections cook rather quickly, and tend to poach in a pan long before a crust can form, exacerbated by the steam-catching gathers formed by the looseness of the grain. The thickest sections can be nicely pan-fried, and the whole thick middle can even be reverse-seared. Most of the recipes that follow are grill recipes, though, since the grill is where the bavette can express its true, delectable self.

BAVETTE WITH TARRAGON AND YELLOW MUSTARD

The tarragon bush in my backyard turns into a monster in July and August, and I'm always looking for ways to use this peculiar and underrated herb. Fresh tarragon has the pinch of anise and the warmth of basil, and it goes very well with steak, under the right circumstances. Grilling it with a big bavette covered in yellow mustard is one of those right circumstances. The mustardy crust will lose the vinegary taste but keep enough tang to bring out the special flavour of tarragon. It makes for a terrific summertime steak for a crowd (or just for you, ending up with brilliant leftovers).

¼ CUP YELLOW MUSTARD
1 TABLESPOON EXTRA-VIRGIN OLIVE OIL
1 BUNCH OF FRESH TARRAGON LEAVES, ROUGHLY CHOPPED (ABOUT 1/2 CUP)
PINCH OF SALT
1 WHOLE BAVETTE STEAK (ABOUT 3 POUNDS)
CRUSHED DRIED CHILIES (LIKE ÁRBOL CHILIES)

SERVES 4 TO 6

IN A BOWL, combine mustard, olive oil, tarragon, and salt. Using your hands, rub the mixture all over your bavette until well coated. Starting at a short end, roll the steak up like a sleeping bag. Set aside at room temperature while you prepare your grill.

PREPARE YOUR CHARCOAL GRILL to one-third cooler than peak heat, or heat your gas grill to medium-high (preheated on High for 10 minutes, lid closed). For charcoal, the coals should be almost all whitened, and you should be able to bear holding your hand 4 inches above the grill for a little more than 2 seconds. This is hotter than usual, but bavette can take the heat, and the grill will cool down as you cook, giving you a chance to turn that mustard into a tangy, smoky crust.

YOU HAVE THE OPTION now of cooking the bavette whole or cutting it in half crosswise.

GRILL YOUR BAVETTE, flipping as needed, until the crust begins to darken and the steak reaches an internal temperature approaching 125°F in the middle. You can also check your steak for doneness with a small incision: juices should flow from a medium-rare

(pinky-red) centre. Remember, the ends will be more done than the middle, and that's okay—there will be lots of steak of varying doneness to go around. When your steak is done, let it rest loosely wrapped in foil for at least 10 minutes.

TO SLICE YOUR STEAK, cut it in half widthwise with a sharp knife (unless you've done this before grilling), then rotate the steak so that the grain runs perpendicular to your knife. Cut it in 1/4-inch slices on a bias away from you to maximize the surface area of each slice.

SERVE sprinkled with a pinch of crushed dried chilies, for colour and the occasional peppery bite.

DUCK-FATTED BAVETTE
WITH SMOKED PAPRIKA

GRILL

Paprika and meat have a long history together. Whether in cured sausage or goulash, the paprika and the meat become one. I think fat has something to do with this tasty ménage, and duck fat works exceptionally well. If you don't have any, you can use lard or a combination of softened butter and olive oil. The result in any case is a rich and rustic smoky steak that is a thrill to grill and a delight to devour.

1 WHOLE BAVETTE STEAK (ABOUT 3 POUNDS)
1 TEASPOON SALT
1 TABLESPOON DUCK FAT
1/2 TEASPOON SMOKED PAPRIKA
FRESHLY GROUND BLACK PEPPER

SERVES 4 TO 6

SEASON YOUR BAVETTE with salt (about 1/2 teaspoon per side). Let sit at room temperature for 30 minutes.

IN A BOWL, or right there on your butcher's paper, work duck fat and smoked paprika into a paste. Using your hands, rub it all over the steak. Starting at a short end, roll up the steak like a sleeping bag. Set aside while you prepare your grill.

PREPARE YOUR CHARCOAL GRILL to one-third cooler than peak heat, or heat your gas grill to medium-high (preheated on High for 10 minutes, lid closed). For charcoal, the coals should be almost all whitened, and you should be able to bear holding your hand 4 inches above the grill for a little more than 2 seconds. This is hotter than usual, but bavette can take the heat, and the grill will cool down as you cook, helping you create a mouth-watering, ducky paprika crust.

YOU HAVE THE OPTION now of cooking the bavette whole or cutting it in half crosswise.

GRILL YOUR BAVETTE, flipping as needed, until the crust begins to darken and the steak reaches an internal temperature approaching 125°F in the middle. You can also check your steak for doneness with a small incision: juices should flow from a medium-rare (pinky-red) centre. Remember, the ends will be more done than the middle, and that's okay—there will be lots of steak of varying degrees of doneness to go around. When your steak is done, let it rest loosely wrapped in foil for at least 10 minutes.

TO SLICE THE STEAK, cut it in half widthwise with a sharp knife (unless you've done this before grilling), then rotate the steak so that the grain runs perpendicular to your knife. Cut it in 1/4-inch slices on a bias away from you to maximize the surface area of each slice.

SERVE the slices laid out on a platter or right on your carving board, seasoned with a few grinds of pepper.

BAVETTE MADEIRA

FRY

You will need some beef stock for this classic French bistro steak recipe (so see page 107, or buy the best you can find, which usually means house-made and frozen from your butcher or a good grocery store). If you can't find Madeira, a rather tasty Portuguese fortified wine, you can use a medium-sweet sherry. Stick a candle in an empty wine bottle, turn on some Edith Piaf, and be the poet musing somewhere in *le dixième arrondissement*. Try serving with parsnip-potato mash, like the one detailed on pages 159–160).

SERVES 2

2 TABLESPOONS UNSALTED BUTTER, DIVIDED
1 SHALLOT, FINELY DICED
3 TO 4 CREMINI MUSHROOMS, THINLY SLICED
1 TABLESPOON ALL-PURPOSE FLOUR
1 CUP BEEF STOCK (AT ROOM TEMPERATURE OR WARMER)
1 CUP MADEIRA WINE
1 ORANGE, FOR ZESTING
SALT AND PEPPER
2 BAVETTE STEAKS (ABOUT 6 OUNCES EACH, PREFERABLY CUT FROM THE THICK MIDDLES)
OLIVE OIL, FOR FRYING

IN A HEAVY FRYING PAN over medium heat, melt 1 tablespoon butter. Add shallot and cook until translucent and softened. Add mushrooms and continue cooking until vegetables turn golden brown. Through a fine-mesh sieve, sprinkle in the flour, stirring continuously until combined. Gradually stir in beef stock. Simmer for 10 to 15 minutes, until the sauce thickens and shines. Stir in Madeira, remaining 1 tablespoon butter, and three zests of the orange (using a Microplane or fine-tooth grater), and simmer for 5 minutes. Season to taste, then remove from heat, keeping warm in a sauce boat or a bowl.

GIVE THE PAN A QUICK WIPE with a paper towel and place over medium-high heat. Melt just enough butter with olive oil to liberally coat the bottom of the pan. Cook your bavette, moving it around the pan to help it develop a crust and flipping as often as you like, until it reaches an internal temperature approaching 120°F, which is just under medium-rare (about 8 minutes total). If you check for doneness with a small incision, the steak will be pinky-red inside, with some running juices, and some rare meat in the middle. Remove from heat. Let your steak rest very loosely wrapped in foil for 5 minutes.

SERVE smothered in the zesty Madeira pan sauce.

BAVETTE WITH CORIANDER CRUST

GRILL

• •

Of all the traditional ways to dry and preserve beef, South African biltong is one of the most interesting. All of the recipes I've tried have used coriander as the primary flavouring agent, and true believers insist on sourcing the spice only from South Africa (though I've never been able to notice that much of a difference). Either way, there is something about beef and coriander that really works, lending the meat a grassy, roasty flavour that seems like it was meant to be. This biltong-inspired recipe does depend on coriander, so you will need to get some if you don't have any in your cupboard. You won't regret having it around.

SERVES 4 TO 6

1 WHOLE BAVETTE STEAK (ABOUT 3 POUNDS)
1 TEASPOON SALT
3 TABLESPOONS WHOLE CORIANDER SEEDS,
  CRUSHED
1 TABLESPOON OLIVE OIL
FRESHLY GROUND BLACK PEPPER

• •

SEASON YOUR BAVETTE with salt (about 1/2 teaspoon per side). Using your hands, press crushed coriander seeds evenly all over the surface of the steak and drizzle with olive oil. Starting with a short end, roll up the steak like a sleeping bag. Let sit while you prepare your grill.

PREPARE YOUR CHARCOAL GRILL to one-third cooler than peak heat, or heat your gas grill to medium-high (preheated on High for 10 minutes, lid closed). For charcoal, the coals should be almost all whitened, and you should be able to bear holding your hand 4 inches above the grill for a little more than 2 seconds. This is hotter than usual, but bavette can take the heat. The grill will cool down as you cook, which will help you create a mouth-watering coriander crust.

YOU HAVE THE OPTION now of cooking the bavette whole or cutting it in half crosswise.

GRILL YOUR BAVETTE, flipping as needed, until the crust begins to darken and the steak reaches an internal temperature approaching 125°F in the middle. You can also check your steak for doneness with a small incision: juices should flow from a medium-rare (pinky-red) centre. Remember, the ends will be more

done than the middle, and that's okay—there will be lots of steak of varying degrees of doneness to go around. When your steak is done, let it rest loosely wrapped in foil for at least 10 minutes.

TO SLICE THE STEAK, cut it in half widthwise with a sharp knife (unless you've done this before grilling), then rotate the steak so that the grain runs perpendicular to your knife. Cut it in 1/4-inch slices on a bias away from you to maximize the surface area of each slice.

SERVE your steak slices laid out on a platter with juices from the foil poured on top, and a few grinds of pepper.

TIP: You can crush the coriander seeds using a mortar and pestle, blender, or spice grinder. You want to end up with a mixture of fine and coarse grains, so if you are using a blender or spice grinder, grind accordingly.

HONEY-GLAZED BAVETTE WITH CHIPOTLE YOGURT

GRILL

Just a small amount of honey infused in melted butter and grilled into a dark, sticky crust transforms a bavette into something altogether different. Amazingly, the taste of actual honey (as opposed to just sweetness) is still detectable. This treatment picks up smoky flavours readily, so if you do have the wherewithal to have some soaked wood chips on hand and ready to add to the fire, it's well worth the effort. The crispy parts of the crust and the surprising soupçon of charred honey are a perfect match for smoky, tangy, creamy chipotle yogurt. If you can look up long enough from your plate, you will see your dinner guests licking theirs.

1/4 CUP UNSALTED BUTTER

1 TABLESPOON LIQUID HONEY

1/4 TEASPOON SALT

1 WHOLE BAVETTE STEAK (ABOUT 3 POUNDS)

2 TO 4 CANNED CHIPOTLE PEPPERS IN ADOBO SAUCE, TO TASTE

1 CUP FULL-FAT (10% OR HIGHER) PLAIN GREEK-STYLE YOGURT

SERVES 4 TO 6

IN A SMALL SAUCEPAN, combine butter, honey, and salt and heat until the butter is melted, stirring occasionally.

POUR HALF of the honey butter onto one side of your bavette and, using your hands, rub it in a little; repeat on the other side (the cool steak will cause the butter to recongeal, and that's okay). Starting with a short end, roll the bavette up like a sleeping bag. Set aside while you prepare the chipotle yogurt and your grill.

IN A BOWL, using a fork, squash chipotle peppers (2 to 4, depending on how peppery you like things) and some of their sauce. Add yogurt and mix well. Taste and adjust if necessary. Transfer mixture to a small bowl and set aside.

PREPARE YOUR CHARCOAL GRILL to one-third cooler than peak heat, or heat your gas grill to medium-high (preheated on High for 10 minutes, lid closed). For charcoal, the coals should be almost all whitened, and you should be able to bear holding your hand 4 inches above the grill for a little more than 2 seconds. This is hotter than usual, but bavette can

take the heat. The grill will cool down as you cook, and you will be able to bring the bavette to medium-rare while creating a lovely crust.

GRILL YOUR BAVETTE, flipping as needed, until the crust begins to darken and the steak reaches an internal temperature approaching 125°F in the middle. You can also check your steak for doneness with a small incision: juices should flow from a medium-rare (pinky-red) centre. Remember, the ends will be more done than the middle, and that's okay—there will be lots of steak of varying degrees of doneness to go around. When your steak is done, let it rest loosely wrapped in foil for at least 10 minutes.

TO SLICE THE STEAK, cut it in half widthwise with a sharp knife, then rotate the steak so that the grain runs perpendicular to your knife. Cut it in 1/4-inch slices on a bias away from you to maximize the surface area of each slice.

SERVE the slices laid out on a platter or on your carving board, with the chipotle yogurt in a small bowl on the side.

CHOPPED STEAK CHEESEBURGER WITH BACON AND ONIONS

Eating a cheeseburger with hand-chopped beef (instead of ground beef) is like having a hundred tiny steaks stuck together in a loose harmony of unctuousness. Miraculously, the meat will stick together almost as well as a finer grind (because meat proteins, and the enzymes that accompany them, are sticky), giving you a burger that simply outclasses all pretenders. The cheese melts its way into the looser texture of the patty, and more fat remains in the food, instead of on the coals or in the pan, which means your burger is juicier, can be made thicker, and has a way better chance of developing a tasty, crispier crust. The mustard I tell you about on page 164 will make this uber-burger even more mind blowing.

3 STRIPS BACON

1 MEDIUM ONION, SLICED INTO THIN ROUNDS

6 OUNCES FATTY CHUCK STEAK, FROZEN
    UNTIL MEAT BEGINS TO CRYSTALLIZE BUT
    IS NOT YET SOLID

GOOD MELTING CHEESE (MEDIUM-OLD
    CHEDDAR OR GRUYÈRE), SHREDDED

THE NICEST SOFT BUN YOU CAN FIND

MAKES 1 BURGER

IN A DRY FRYING PAN, fry bacon until medium crisp. Transfer to a plate lined in paper towel. Pour excess fat from pan into a coffee cup, ramekin, or other heatproof vessel, reserving a little to fry onions.

IN THE SAME PAN over medium heat, fry onion until soft and golden, about 4 minutes. Transfer to a bowl and set aside. Wipe pan with a paper towel.

USING A SHARP KNIFE, cut your partially frozen, fatty chuck into 1/4-inch strips. Chop those strips into 1/4-inch pieces (or smaller). Chop 1 strip bacon into bits and add to chopped chuck. Using your hands, mix everything together and form into 1/2-inch-thick patty.

HEAT THE SAME PAN over medium-high heat. Press the patty gently onto the surface of the pan (some bits of meat may fall away from the patty, but that's okay; it all goes on the bun). Cook for 3 minutes or until the patty is appropriately dark and crusted, then flip over. Place grated cheese on top and let melt as your patty continues to cook for another 3 to 4 minutes to medium, or above 135°F.

SERVE cheesy chopped steak in your soft bun garnished with remaining 2 strips of bacon and fried onions.

CHOPPING YOUR OWN BEEF

Chopping your own beef gives you the opportunity to choose exactly what goes into your patty. My favourite beef for hand chopping is fatty chuck because of its bold beefy flavour and ample, soft fat. Brisket and short rib work well, too. The trick to good chopping: use partially frozen meat, large pieces (as in, a whole piece of steak), and a heavy, sharp knife. Cleavers are great, and a chef's knife will do just fine. The process makes a bit of a mess, but what the taste and texture does to the pleasure centre of your brain makes everything okay. Once you chop your own beef, there is no going back.

TRI-TIP

TENDERNESS: moderately tender up to medium-rare
GRAIN: coarse, dense grain runs across the length of the steak
from the top short point to the long point of this triangular muscle
FAT: quite lean, with scant streaks of fat running with the grain
KEY FEATURES: similar to a sirloin in texture, if somewhat
less tender after medium-rare; nice shape, easy to carve

I must admit it took me a while to get around to appreciating the tri-tip, but appreciate it I do. Taken from the bottom of the sirloin near the leg of the animal, it is a somewhat tougher and leaner cut than a top sirloin. It is a single, triangular muscle, responsible for moving and stabilizing the knee cap, so it does quite a lot of work for the live beast.

It's a large steak when it is kept whole, but not overly so. I recommend cooking it whole since it is easiest to carve it that way: cutting it across its width will get you nicely shaped, across-the-grain slices. In most cases the tri-tip will be the cheapest steak in the shop. If you can resist eating the whole thing for dinner, any leftovers are perfect the next day for lunch.

The leanness of this steak makes it an ideal candidate for brining, and also for barbecue-style crusts. The brine really helps the meat pick up the grill flavours, and prominent, barbecue-inspired sauces give the tri-tip a taste of California (where the tri-tip first became popular in the United States).

Pre-salting your meat not only adds flavour; it also helps the meat hold on to moisture because it denatures some of the meat protein. Brining penetrates more deeply into the meat, helping lean, less moist cuts like the tri-tip hold on to their precious juices. You can certainly cook a tri-tip without a brine (especially if you reverse-sear it), but for the grill, I love the results of brining.

TRI-TIP WITH
PRESERVED LEMON-CHILI DRY RUB AND YOGURT SAUCE

I've called for dried preserved lemon in this recipe because the flavour is unbelievably good. It is a little hard to find, though—try Middle Eastern shops and look for whole, dried lemons. If you can't find them, dust the steak with the zest of one lemon just before you rest the steak in foil. In any case, this is a terrific way to enjoy tri-tip. The smoky, piquant flavour of the crust marries the brined meat and tangy yogurt dip perfectly.

SERVES 4 TO 6

4 CUPS WATER

4 TABLESPOONS CELTIC-STYLE SEA SALT OR NATURAL ROCK SALT

1 WHOLE TRI-TIP STEAK (ABOUT 2 POUNDS)

1 TABLESPOON OLIVE OIL, FOR FRYING

1 MEDIUM ONION, THINLY SLICED

JUICE OF 1/4 LEMON

2 DRIED PRESERVED LEMONS (GROUND WITH A SPICE GRINDER OR BLENDER)

2 TABLESPOONS GROUND DRIED ANCHO CHILI

1 TEASPOON GROUND CORIANDER

1 TEASPOON GROUND CUMIN

1/4 TEASPOON GROUND CINNAMON

1 CUP (OR MORE) FULL-FAT (3.5 TO 4%) YOGURT

MAKE THE QUICK BRINE: In a large bowl or baking dish, dissolve salt in water. Add your whole tri-tip steak, making sure it is fully submerged (if not, make another small batch of salt-water brine). Cover and let sit at room temperature for at least 1 hour.

MEANWHILE, in a frying pan over medium heat, heat olive oil. Add onions, season with a pinch of salt, and cook until golden brown. Add lemon juice and continue cooking until lemon juice completely evaporates, about 1 minute. Set pan aside.

IN A SMALL BOWL, combine preserved lemon and spices. Using your hands, evenly coat steak in spice mixture. Reserve leftover spices. Set steak aside.

PREPARE YOUR CHARCOAL GRILL to one-third cooler than peak heat, or heat your gas grill to medium-high (preheated on High for 10 minutes, lid closed). This is a thick steak that will ball up and get thicker as you cook it, so with long barbecue tongs or a grill rake, move the coals as much as you can to one side of the grill, leaving the other side less hot and

partially out of direct heat. For gas grills, simply turn off one side of the grill.

GRILL YOUR STEAK on the hotter side, waiting until the steak releases its grip on the grill before turning it. Do this again for the second side, then move it to the cooler side of the grill and close the lid.

CHECK THE TRI-TIP every 4 minutes, and remove from heat as it reaches 120°F (this is a lean steak, and not sufficiently engorged to stay juicy much after that). Lightly dust all over with reserved rub (if you are using lemon zest instead of preserved lemon, now is the time to sprinkle your steak with it). Let steak rest very loosely wrapped in foil for 10 minutes.

MEANWHILE, in a small bowl, combine lemony onions with yogurt.

USING A SHARP KNIFE, cut your tri-tip into 1/4-inch slices across the grain (along its width). Serve with tangy yogurt dip.

SMOKE IT UP!

For an amazing extra punch of cherry smoke, soak bits of cherry wood in water for half an hour, then toss them on your hot coals when you close the barbecue lid. For gas grills, wrap the wood in aluminum foil, puncture it in a few places so smoke can escape, and place the pouch directly on the heating plate or a very hot part of the grill until it begins to smoke, then close the hood. You can buy cherry wood pellets at better barbecue retailers (or use your own wood chips or twigs, if you have them). The smoke won't last long, but a little goes a long way.

CHERRY-GRILLED TRI-TIP

GRILL

My neighbour has an enormous cherry tree in his back yard. It is so large that he regularly prunes substantial limbs from it and then drops off cherry wood at my house, which I gratefully accept and use to give extra flavour to my food when I'm grilling or smoking. This also means I get the occasional cherry harvest from him, either already in a mason jar full of rum, waiting to be opened and enjoyed come December, or just a bagful of cherries. When that happens, I use some of them to make what I think is a knock-down good barbecue sauce, which is terrific on ribs, brisket, and tri-tip—especially brined tri-tip.

SERVES 4 TO 6

4 CUPS WATER

4 TABLESPOONS CELTIC-STYLE SEA SALT OR NATURAL ROCK SALT

1 WHOLE TRI-TIP STEAK (2 TO 2 1/2 POUNDS)

2 POUNDS CHERRIES, PITTED (SEE TIP)

1/4 CUP WATER

1/2 TEASPOON GROUND NUTMEG

1/4 TEASPOON GROUND CINNAMON

3/4 CUP LIQUID HONEY

JUICE OF 1/4 LEMON

PINCH OF SALT, OR TO TASTE

MAKE THE QUICK BRINE: In a large bowl or baking dish, dissolve salt in water. Add your whole tri-tip steak, making sure it is fully submerged (if not, make another small batch of salt-water brine). Cover and let sit at room temperature for at least 1 hour.

MEANWHILE, in a saucepan over medium-low heat, combine cherries, water, nutmeg, and cinnamon. Simmer until cherries have completely lost their shape and the sauce begins to thicken. Add honey and continue to simmer, reducing the heat as necessary when the thick sauce starts to splutter. Add lemon juice and salt. Taste and adjust seasonings until you have a sauce that you adore. Using an immersion blender, purée mixture until smooth (alternatively, you can push the sauce through a fine-mesh sieve using the back of a spoon). The whole process should take about 25 minutes.

PREPARE YOUR CHARCOAL GRILL to one-third cooler than peak heat, or heat your gas grill to medium-high (preheated on High for 10 minutes, lid closed). This is a thick steak that will ball up and get thicker as you cook it, so with long barbecue tongs or a grill rake, move the coals as much as you can to one side of the grill, leaving the other side less hot and partially out of direct heat. For gas grills, simply turn off one side of the grill.

SMOTHER YOUR TRI-TIP in cherry sauce, reserving 1/2 cup, and grill on the hotter side, waiting until the steak releases its grip on the grill before turning it. Do this again for the second side, then move it to the cooler side of the grill and close the lid.

CHECK YOUR TRI-TIP every 4 minutes, and remove from heat as it reaches 120°F (this is a lean steak, and not sufficiently engorged to stay juicy much after that). Slather more sauce on the steak, then let steak rest very loosely wrapped in foil for 10 minutes.

SLICE YOUR STEAK across the grain and serve with a side of sauce mixed with foil juices.

TIP: Wondering if you can use canned cherries? You certainly can. Just make sure you use the juice for the sauce too, cooking it down exactly as you would with fresh cherries.

GRILLED BLOODY MARY

I can't think of a more appropriate pre-steak cocktail than a grilled bloody Mary. Consider it a boozy appetizer in a glass. Better still, you can make them right at your grill, which is of course one of the best places to be on any given occasion.

1 LEMON, CUT INTO 1-INCH SLICES,
    FOR RIMMING GLASS
CELERY SALT, FOR RIMMING GLASS
1 JUMBO SHRIMP (PEELED, DEVEINED,
    AND TAIL INTACT)
OLIVE OIL, FOR COOKING
YOUR FAVOURITE HOT SAUCE
1 NICE PICKLE (SEE PAGE 89)
1 SCALLION
ICE CUBES
1 1/2 OUNCES VODKA
1/2 OUNCE DRY VERMOUTH
TOMATO JUICE
2 TO 3 CAPERS

SERVES 1

MOISTEN the rim of a tall glass with a slice of lemon, then twist the rim of the glass in a plate of celery salt, to coat. Set aside.

BRUSH your prepared shrimp with a little olive oil and hot sauce, and grill alongside pickle and scallion (not oiled), until the shrimp is pink and begins to curl, the pickle picks up grill marks, and the scallion chars at the ends.

FILL the glass with ice, then carefully pour in vodka and vermouth. Top up with tomato juice, leaving some room for the garnishes to displace the liquid, and gently stir. Garnish with grilled shrimp, scallion, and pickle as well as capers and a dash of your favourite hot sauce.

PRIME RIB

TENDERNESS: very tender
GRAIN: medium-to-fine grain runs top to bottom
though the steak, and across the steak at the rib-eye cap
FAT: well marbled throughout, with clusters of fat in parts, and a sizeable fat cap
KEY FEATURES: tender and forgiving if slightly overcooked;
good from rare to medium; variously textured

Of all the steaks commonly available in North America, the bone-in prime rib steak is my hands-down favourite. Peter Sanagan, the owner of Sanagan's Meat Locker in Toronto's bohemian Kensington Market, and his manager, Brian Knapp, could set a clock to my arrival every Friday evening when I show up seeking the big rib steak I dream of all week.

It is sometimes called bone-in rib eye, cowboy steak, or côte de boeuf, depending on how precise the butcher cares to be about the exact location of the steak along the rib section, and depending on the style of cut. Essentially, though, steaks within ribs 7 through 12, from the back to the front of the animal, are prime rib territory. Further up the beast, you're in the chuck. The muscle groups are mostly the same, but the closer you get to the cow's neck, the tougher the meat becomes. A nice cheat is the very flavourful but less tender blade-eye (or chuck-eye) steak, above rib 12.

Rib steaks are adorned with clusters of eminently meltable fat, a substantial fat cap, and excellent marbling throughout. Tender sections of three muscle groups make up the rib steak, including the incredibly interesting spinalis dorsi, which rims the outer perimeter of the steak with a splendidly loose-textured meat, holding just the right amount of fat to keep it from overcooking while the rest of the steak reaches ideal doneness. Tenderness aside, it is this variety in texture that makes the rib steak such a special treat. I always cook it with the bone attached, carving it off when I cut up the steak for serving. This guards the meat adjacent to the bone against overcooking, and gives you the option of a little more rare steak among the medium-rare, or even medium-cooked steak (rib steak is forgiving enough to let you cook it all the way to medium if you like it that way, without causing a steak tragedy). For optimum deliciousness, though, medium-rare is still the way to go.

SPINALIS DORSI—THE GOLDEN CHILD OF PRIME RIB

When the spinalis dorsi muscle becomes a distinct steak (also known as rib-eye cap, deckle steak, and calotte, which is not to be confused with the completely different *culotte* steak), it's like finding the most flavourful, easy-going steak on the whole cow, then taking just the most tender, splendidly textured, perfectly marbled section. I've special-ordered a whole piece before and actually felt I was committing a steak sin when I grilled it and ate it. It's that good. Try it if you can get your butcher to cut a big enough piece for you (and you really feel like splurging, since they don't come cheap). Whole, the rib-eye cap is 15 to 18 inches long, and half as wide. Grill it on a hot grill and slice it any way you like. It's as tender as a filet, as textured as a bavette, and as buttery as a skirt.

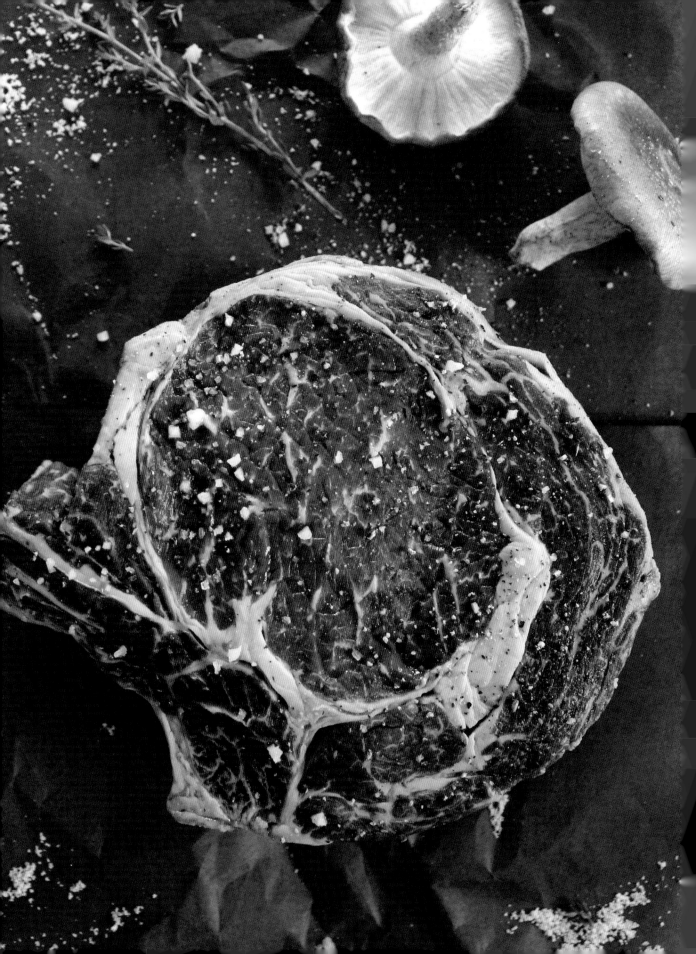

ROASTING RED PEPPERS

Since you're roasting peppers, why not roast a couple of whole peppers, too? They are incredible on sandwiches and will keep in the fridge for a week. Simply add whole peppers to the sheet of foil along with the garlic and peppers. When the garlic is ready, so are the peppers. Let cool, then pinch off the skin (it's okay if a little stays behind). Cut each roasted pepper in half and discard seeds and stalk. Enjoy as is or use in the recipe for the Ultimate Steak Sandwich on page 163.

PRIME RIB STEAK
WITH ROASTED GARLIC AND RED PEPPER MATCHSTICKS

REVERSE-SEAR

This recipe isn't really a whole meal, though I have absolutely eaten it as such with my more carnivorous friends. The vegetable adornments add concentrated flavours that complement the meat perfectly. Look for a steak with a generous fat cap, to render for frying. If your steak is too well trimmed, use a tablespoon of duck fat or lard.

SERVES 4 TO 6

AS MANY RED PEPPERS AS YOU LIKE (OR 1 RED PEPPER FOR EVERY TWO DINNER GUESTS)
AS MANY WHOLE HEADS OF GARLIC AS YOU LIKE (OR 1 HEAD PER DINNER GUEST)
OLIVE OIL, FOR COOKING
1 BIG BONE-IN RIB STEAK, 2 INCHES THICK OR MORE (ABOUT 2 1/2 POUNDS)
1 TEASPOON SALT

PLACE a wire rack on the middle rack of the oven and line the rack below it with enough foil to catch the steak drippings while allowing the steak to bask freely in your oven's dry winds. Preheat your oven to 375°F.

USING A VERY SHARP KNIFE, cut the red peppers into matchsticks. Set aside.

PLACE each head of garlic on a piece of foil large enough to cover it completely. Drizzle garlic with olive oil and sprinkle with a little salt, then wrap snugly.

THINLY COAT a cast-iron pan or baking sheet in olive oil. Place wrapped garlic and red pepper matchsticks on pan, keeping them separate. Bake in preheated oven for 15 minutes, then turn peppers over so they roast evenly. Cook for an additional 10 minutes, or until the peppers are soft but not soggy. (Roasting them this way should get them to dry out before their own juices poach them, so they aren't wilted and have a more concentrated flavour.) Remove pan from oven and set aside. The peppers will hold nicely in the pan, and the garlic will continue to cook a little in the foil. If you find the garlic is not soft enough (when squeezed it should give underneath the foil), leave the pan in the oven as you continue to the next step.

REDUCE OVEN TEMPERATURE to 225°F. Sprinkle steak all over with salt. Place your salted steak on the wire rack (this is a good time to also check on your garlic and remove if ready) and cook in preheated oven for about 30 minutes per pound (about 1 1/2 hours total), turning once halfway through to dry out both sides evenly, until it reaches an internal temperature of 115°F in the meaty middle (that is, not in a seam or in fat, but in the meatiest part of the middle of the steak).

WHEN YOUR STEAK IS READY, remove it from the oven and turn oven off. Place pan of roasted garlic and peppers in oven to warm through.

HEAT a heavy pan (cast iron, stainless steel, or non-stick with a heat-cookie bottom) on high heat until very hot. Using tongs, hold your steak upright, with its fat cap against the pan's surface. Move the steak slowly around the pan until enough fat has rendered to coat it. Sear steak on both sides until a nice, dark brown crust develops and the steak reaches an internal temperature approaching 125°F in the middle.

TRANSFER your steak to a sheet of foil, wrap very loosely, and let rest for 5 to 10 minutes.

USING A SHARP KNIFE, cut off the bone, keeping it just a bit meaty to serve as a lucky prize with the big steak. Cut steak crosswise into 1/4-inch slices. Serve right on the carving board, if your board has a runnel and well, or on a warmed platter. Adorn steak with red pepper matchsticks and roasted garlic, directing your guests to squish the savoury garlic paste from its paper, as a condiment for their steak.

STEAK CANAPÉS

You can cook a steak especially for making these scrumptious canapés or simply use leftovers from a big steak dinner, as I have here. Prime rib, striploin, and tenderloin all work well.

I use crème fraîche to hold everything deliciously in place. Serve these to your guests at teatime or as a seduction before dinner. Garnish them as you please, but I've included some ideas that have gone over pretty well *chez moi* (see photo caption).

VERY NICE BAGUETTE, CUT INTO 1/4-INCH
SLICES
CRÈME FRAÎCHE
COLD, TENDER COOKED STEAK, NEATLY CARVED
INTO 1/8-INCH SLICES
MICROGREENS
SAVOURY GARNISHES (PICKLES, OLIVES,
CHEESE, CAPERS)
YOUR CHOICE OF CONDIMENTS (TAPENADE,
SEEDY MUSTARD, PEPPER JELLY, ETC.)

SLATHER baguette slices with crème fraîche. Top with a single slice of steak, and then another dollop of crème fraîche and a few microgreens. Carefully arrange savoury garnishes and a scant few more greens on top, anchoring everything in place.

TIP: If you're using steak you've just cooked, refrigerate it for at least 2 hours before carving it. Cold steak is much easier to carve into tidy slices, and that is what you want for these delectable little works of art.

From left to right: 1) Old cheddar cheese, pimento-stuffed olives, seedy mustard, pea shoots. 2) Camembert cheese, capers, habanero pepper jelly, broccoli sprouts. 3) Boiled quail egg, Munster cheese, scallions, smoked paprika. 4) Caper berries, quick-pickled onion slices in beet brine, pea shoots. 5) Tomatillo salsa, sweet pickled tomatoes, arugula shoots.

RIB STEAK WITH
BROWN-BUTTER PARSNIP MASH AND CARAMELIZED LEEKS

REVERSE-SEAR

This dish is a something of a royal feast. Your kitchen will smell like the best steakhouse in the world, your guests will be drooling in anticipation, and they won't be let down. The happy truth is that this meal is easy to make thanks to its well-timed method, which means you can quite reliably cook everything at once.

1 BIG BONE-IN RIB STEAK, 2 INCHES THICK
   OR MORE (ABOUT 2 1/2 POUNDS)
2 1/2 TEASPOONS SALT, DIVIDED
1/2 CUP UNSALTED BUTTER
2 MEDIUM PARSNIPS, PEELED AND CUT INTO
   1-INCH PIECES
4 MEDIUM YUKON GOLD POTATOES, PEELED
   AND CUT INTO 1-INCH PIECES
2 WHOLE LEEKS

1 TABLESPOON OLIVE OIL, FOR FRYING
UNSALTED BUTTER, FOR FRYING
SALT AND PEPPER, TO TASTE
1 LEMON (MOST FOR ZESTING, 1/4 FOR
   SQUEEZING)
1 CUP HEAVY OR WHIPPING (35%) CREAM (AT
   ROOM TEMPERATURE OR SOMEWHAT WARMER)

SERVES 4 TO 6

PLACE A WIRE RACK on the middle rack of the oven and line the rack below it with enough foil to catch the steak drippings while allowing the steak to bask freely in your oven's dry winds. There won't be much dripping, but this makes cleanup easy and will ensure you don't get a smoky oven the next time you cook at higher temperatures. Preheat your oven to 225°F.

SPRINKLE about 1 teaspoon salt all over your steak. Place your salted steak on the wire rack and cook in preheated oven for about 30 minutes per pound (about 1 1/2 hours total), turning once halfway through to dry out both sides evenly, until it reaches an internal temperature of 115°F in the meaty middle (that is, not in a seam or in fat, but in the meatiest part of the middle of the steak).

MEANWHILE, in a saucepan over medium-low heat, cook butter until all the bubbles have finished erupting, and brown bits of solids begin to form in the pan (the butter should taste rich and nutty). Remove pan from heat immediately and transfer brown butter to a coffee cup or other heatproof vessel.

WHEN YOUR STEAK is 30 minutes from being done in the oven, place prepared parsnips and potatoes in a large saucepan, cover with water, add 1 1/2 teaspoons salt, and boil until fork-tender, about 20 minutes.

MEANWHILE, prepare leeks: Using a sharp knife, trim off roots, then cut leeks into 3- to 4-inch lengths (white and light green parts only). Next, cut them in half lengthwise but keep 1 inch of one end intact, making it easier to free them of their grit and so they don't fall apart (see photo, page 161). Hold the intact end firmly and rinse the leeks well. Heat olive oil in a frying pan over medium-high heat. Place leeks in pan, cut-side up, and dab a knife-point of butter onto each leek. Season liberally with salt and pepper. Cook until leeks start crackling, then carefully turn over. (If you don't see this nice coating when you turn the leeks the first time, continue cooking until you do.) Squeeze lemon overtop. Reduce heat to medium-low, cover, and continue cooking for about 7 minutes, until creamy-soft with a sticky brown coating. Transfer cooked leeks to a serving dish and place in a warm oven, reserving pan for searing steak.

CONTINUED ON NEXT PAGE

ONCE THE POTATOES and parsnips are fork-tender, remove pan from heat. Drain and let steam-dry in the pan for about 5 minutes. Using a potato ricer or food mill, rice vegetables into a large bowl (you could also just mash them, but the ricer or food mill will give you fluffier, less gluey, results). Using a wooden spoon or spatula, fold in heavy cream, a pinch of salt, and reserved brown butter. Transfer to a serving dish and place in warm oven, along with cooked leeks.

HEAT THE RESERVED PAN over medium-high heat. Sear your steak for 30 seconds, and then flip, searing the other side of the steak, flipping again as needed until a nice, dark brown crust develops and the steak reaches an internal temperature approaching 125°F in the middle. Your steak may sear faster than usual, even at this slightly lower temperature, because of the caramelized leek residue in the pan.

TRANSFER seared steak to a sheet of foil, wrap very loosely, and let rest for 5 to 10 minutes.

USING A SHARP KNIFE, cut off the bone, keeping it just a bit meaty to serve as a lucky prize with the big steak. Cut steak crosswise into 1/4-inch slices. Serve right on the carving board, if your board has a runnel and well, or on a warmed platter. Season with salt and pepper to taste, and a little finely grated lemon zest. Serve with warm mash and leeks.

ULTIMATE STEAK SANDWICH
WITH BACON MAYONNAISE

Yup, bacon mayonnaise. I've included this here because prime rib is big, and there are often leftovers after your fabulous feast the night before. Perfectly fine, in my view, and made even better with the prospect of a honking good sandwich the next day for lunch. The key is layering, great bread, and the perfect combination of textures. Mayonnaise, in case you didn't know, is merely whipped-up oil and egg yolk. Here I've made the quite sane decision to replace half of the oil with the bacon fat you'll render from frying the bacon for this sandwich.

MAKES 1 BIG SANDWICH

1 POUND HIGH-QUALITY BACON STRIPS
1 CUP (APPROX.) SUNFLOWER OIL, GRAPESEED OIL, OR OTHER NEUTRAL-TASTING OIL
2 EGG YOLKS
PINCH OF SALT
1 TABLESPOON WHITE WINE VINEGAR, OR TO TASTE
JUICE OF 1/4 LEMON
YOUR FAVOURITE RUSTIC BREAD
LEFTOVER STEAK, THINLY SLICED
3 OR 4 PIECES ROASTED RED BELL PEPPERS (FROM A JAR OR HOMEMADE; SEE PAGE 156)
1/2 CUP SHREDDED CHEDDAR CHEESE
A HANDFUL OF YOUR FAVOURITE GREEN SPROUTS
A BIG LEAF OF STURDY LETTUCE, GENTLY TORN TO THE SIZE OF YOUR BREAD
1 TEASPOON DIJON-STYLE MUSTARD (FROM A JAR OR HOMEMADE, SEE PAGE 164)

IN A DRY FRYING PAN over medium heat, fry bacon until just crisp (but not too well done, to keep it pliable for the sandwich). Remove pan from heat and transfer cooked bacon to a plate lined in paper towel. Let fat cool in pan for 5 minutes, and then drain into a coffee cup or other heatproof vessel. Let cool for another 5 to 10 minutes. Measure out cooled bacon fat (you should have about 1 cup). Pour into a bowl and stir in neutral oil. (If you have less than 1 cup bacon fat, just top it up with oil. You should end up with 2 cups total.)

IN A MIXING BOWL, whisk together egg yolks and salt until frothy, then slowly whisk in half of the oil mixture. Whisk until thickened, then whisk in vinegar and remaining oil mixture. Squeeze in lemon juice and mix to combine. Taste and adjust vinegar and lemon juice as desired.

ASSEMBLE YOUR SANDWICHES: Slather mayonnaise, to taste, on slices of bread and layer bacon and the remaining ingredients to make a sandwich. Don't be afraid to slather a bit more mayo between the layers, and stack the sandwich as tall as you like. You can use toothpicks to hold the sandwich together. (You will probably have some bacon left over if you're just making one sandwich.) Transfer the leftover mayo to a jar or sealable container and keep in the fridge for up to 10 days.

SERVE sandwich with a skewered pickle, if you like (see page 89).

MUSTARD

Among the sauces and condiments that can adorn a bite of steak, a really good mustard can turn that already knee-weakening mouthful into something positively swoony. One afternoon while my friend and frequent food collaborator Ivy Knight and I were eating our way through the lunch menu at the Drake Commissary in Toronto's west end, I had an opportunity to sample chef Ben Bergero's mustard, made with the fine beer from Henderson Brewery next door. I dabbed a little onto my forkful of brisket, and Ivy laughed out loud at my reaction, my eyes the size of dinner plates, my face slackened in bliss. The Drake Commissary was kind enough to give me their recipe. There is a 60-day aging process here, but trust me, it is all worth it. The mustard may be chef Ben Bergero's, but the bragging rights will be at least half your own.

HENDERSON'S BEST MUSTARD

1 CUP YELLOW MUSTARD SEEDS

1 CUP BROWN MUSTARD SEEDS

2 CUPS ALE, PREFERABLY HENDERSON'S BEST
(500 ML TALL-BOY CAN)

1/4 CUP KEEN'S MUSTARD POWDER

1/2 CUP FINELY DICED SPANISH ONION

5 TEASPOONS GRANULATED SUGAR

3 TABLESPOONS KOSHER SALT

3 TEASPOONS BLACK PEPPERCORNS, TOASTED
AND FINELY GROUND (ABOUT 2 1/2 TSP
GROUND)

9 TABLESPOONS PURE MAPLE SYRUP
(PREFERABLY FROM PRINCE EDWARD COUNTY)

5 TEASPOONS APPLE CIDER VINEGAR (PREFER-
ABLY RAW AND UNPASTEURIZED)

MAKES ABOUT 5 1/2 CUPS

IN A BOWL, soak yellow and brown mustard seeds in beer overnight. The next day, add mustard powder, finely diced onions, sugar, salt, and ground pepper. Cover and set aside in a cool place (the fridge works well here) for at least 30 days.

USING A BLENDER, purée half of the mustard seed mixture until smooth. Return mustard seed purée to the remaining mixture and stir in maple syrup and cider vinegar. Cover and refrigerate for 30 more days.

TASTE AND ADJUST salt, syrup, and vinegar as it suits you. Serve with smoked or grilled meats.

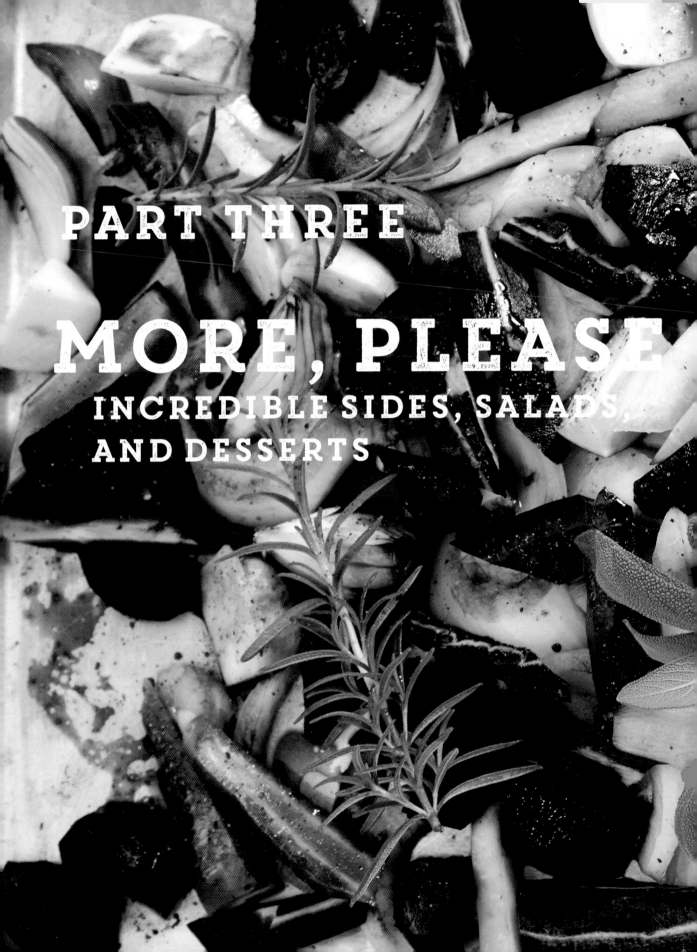

PART THREE

MORE, PLEASE
INCREDIBLE SIDES, SALADS, AND DESSERTS

SIDES

WHEN YOUR FRIENDS RECALL THAT WONDERFUL NIGHT YOU MADE THAT PERFECT STEAK DINNER, IT FEELS PRETTY GOOD. BUT IF THEY REMEMBER THE INCREDIBLE SALAD AND THE PERFECTLY RENDERED POTATOES ON TOP OF THAT, WELL THEN, YOU'VE REALLY DONE SOMETHING. HERE ARE SOME SPECTACULAR SALADS AND SIDE DISHES THAT I'VE HAD SUCCESS WITH OVER THE YEARS AND THAT HAVE BECOME NATURAL PARTNERS TO STEAK AT MY HOUSE.

ASPARAGUS THREE WAYS

As seasonal as I claim to be, there comes a point sometime in March when I would kill for a fresh-cut vegetable. Asparagus is the first to arrive, but I can never resist buying imports a few weeks earlier than our fabulous Ontario harvest allows for in June. The earlier the cut, the thicker the stalks. I love fat, juicy, candlestick-sized asparagus, and I'm careful to peel the skin from the lower third so I don't have to cut much of the end away and I can enjoy every tender morsel. I eat asparagus until the pencil-sized spears peter out in July.

Here I give you what I think are the three best ways to bring out the best of this vegetable: brined and grilled, blanched, and pan-fried.

BRINED AND GRILLED ASPARAGUS

Before grilling your asparagus, try brining it in salty water. The asparagus will stay greener and a little firmer than raw asparagus would, and the salt complements the taste of the grill. For this recipe, you can either cut your asparagus in half lengthwise or leave it whole.

1 TEASPOON SALT PER 1 CUP LUKEWARM WATER
1 BUNCH OF ASPARAGUS, RINSED WELL

SERVES 4

IN A LARGE BOWL, combine water and salt and stir until water is dissolved. Add asparagus, cover, and let sit at room temperature for 20 minutes (a little longer won't hurt them).

HEAT GRILL to medium-high or hotter. Arrange asparagus perpendicular to the rungs of your grill. Grill just until asparagus darkens slightly and bends slightly when you pick it up with kitchen tongs. Serve with a splash of nice olive oil or a pat of butter.

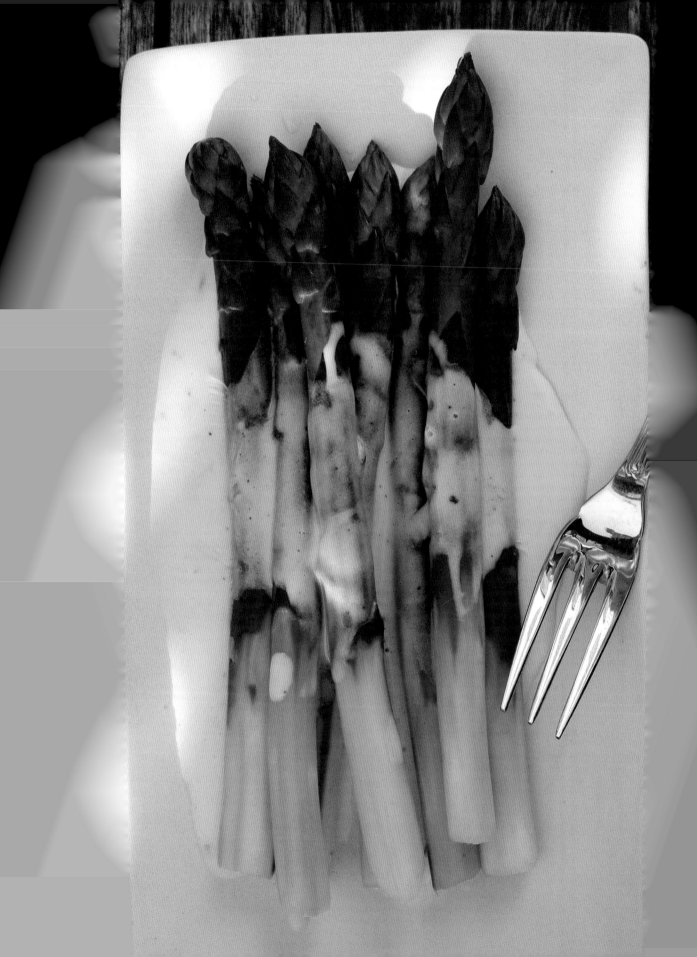

BLANCHED ASPARAGUS WITH BÉARNAISE SAUCE

A classic preparation, this asparagus is marvellous served at room temperature, under a blanket of Béarnaise sauce. Béarnaise is a close cousin to hollandaise, one of the "mother sauces" of French cuisine. Essentially, it is an emulsion of butter fat and raw egg yolks, infused with shallot and enhanced with tarragon and lemon or vinegar. My version isn't quite classic, but it is very close, and in my view as good or better (and quite a bit easier).

SERVES 2 TO 4

1 BUNCH OF ASPARAGUS, RINSED WELL
1 TEASPOON SALT PER 1 CUP WATER

BÉARNAISE SAUCE
1/2 POUND UNSALTED BUTTER
1 SMALL SHALLOT, FINELY DICED
3 EGG YOLKS (AT ROOM TEMPERATURE)
JUICE OF 1/4 LEMON
3 SPRIGS FRESH TARRAGON, COARSELY CHOPPED
SALT

USING A SHARP KNIFE, trim each asparagus stalk 1/8 inch from the cut end. If you feel the knife pulling at woody fibre, cut off another 1/8 inch. Using a Y-shaped vegetable peeler, gently peel the lower third of each asparagus stalk (a light swipe four or five times while turning the stalk should do the trick).

HAVE A LARGE BOWL of ice water at the ready, to shock the asparagus after boiling and preserve their colour.

BRING A WIDE SAUCEPAN or frying pan filled with enough water to cover all of the asparagus to a boil (but don't add the asparagus just yet). Generously salt the water (salt will keep asparagus a brighter green and help with texture and flavour; there's no need to salt the finished dish). Once the water reaches a rolling boil, carefully add asparagus and boil for just 3 minutes.

USING KITCHEN TONGS, test one stalk for doneness by either taking a bite or bending it with your fingers. The asparagus should be firm and bouncy, with only the slightest hint of crunch left. If you are testing it by hand, you should be able to bend the stalk about 60 degrees without breaking it. If it's still crunchy, boil for another 30 seconds to 1 minute. Using tongs, immediately plunge the cooked asparagus into the prepared ice bath for 2 minutes.

TRANSFER asparagus to a clean kitchen towel when ready to make the Béarnaise.

TO MAKE THE BÉARNAISE, melt the butter in a pan on medium heat until it bubbles, and then add the shallot and tarragon. Cook until the butter has mostly stopped bubbling, about 45 seconds. Be careful not to brown the shallots. Strain the butter (now partially "clarified") into a mug or other heatproof vessel, and allow to cool almost to room temperature. Discard the shallot and tarragon.

FILL A MIXING BOWL with hot tap water and set aside for 2 to 3 minutes, until the bowl holds enough heat to keep it warm for a while. Discard the water, wipe the bowl dry, and then add the egg yolks and whisk until smooth. Whisk in the melted butter a tablespoon or so at a time, until the sauce thickens to a custard-like consistency. Squeeze in the lemon and whisk to combine. Season with salt to taste.

TRANSFER the asparagus to a platter. Top with warm Béarnaise sauce and serve immediately.

PAN-FRIED ASPARAGUS

· ·

Pan-frying works exceptionally well for truly thin, end-of-season asparagus. If your asparagus is too thin to peel, just cut off the woody ends.

SERVES 4

1 BUNCH OF ASPARAGUS, RINSED WELL
1 TEASPOON UNSALTED BUTTER
1 TEASPOON OLIVE OIL, FOR FRYING
PINCH OF SALT
2 SPRIGS THYME
1 CLOVE GARLIC, SMASHED

· ·

USING A SHARP KNIFE, trim each asparagus stalk 1/8 inch from the cut end. If you feel the knife pulling at woody fibre, cut off another 1/8 inch. Using a Y-shaped vegetable peeler, gently peel the lower third of each asparagus stalk (a light swipe four or five times while turning the stalk should do the trick).

IN A FRYING PAN over medium-high heat, combine butter, olive oil, and salt. Once the butter's bubbling slows, add asparagus, thyme, and garlic. Sauté until just fork-tender (the asparagus tips should slightly darken and asparagus should turn a brighter shade of green in general).

SERVE ON A PLATTER, along with the cooked clove of smashed garlic for whoever is fast enough to grab it first.

RICE THREE WAYS

I make rice often because it is easy to cook, easy to manipulate, and lets me get on to other things. It also tastes terrific, once you get into different varieties. I stopped using white rice a long time ago, much preferring different sorts of brown rice like brown basmati, and other long- and short-grain varieties. Brown rice is tastier and certainly more nutritious. It is also more forgiving if it's overdone, readily reparable if it's underdone, and has a more satisfying texture when it's cooked just right. (See sidebar on page 177.)

Once you get going with rice, you may want to start adding other grains to the mix: a little farro, pot barley (also fantastic on its own, with this same, simple cooking method), wild rice, wheat berries, kamut, or other exotic rice varieties like black rice and red rice. The grains tend to be chewier when cooked at the same time, but that only adds texture. If you find you want a more uniform bite, soak the grains in water for 30 minutes before you add your rice and start the boil.

BROWN BUTTER RICE

• •

Browning butter adds a wonderful nutty, toasted toffee flavour to rice. The process is necessarily quick, and easy once you get the hang of it.

1 CUP RICE
1/2 CUP UNSALTED BUTTER
SALT

SERVES 4

• •

IN A LARGE SAUCEPAN, cook rice (see instructions opposite).

MEANWHILE, in a pan over medium heat, melt butter until it stops bubbling. When the butter browns and small flecks start to appear in the buttery mass, remove pan from the heat and immediately pour the butter into a coffee cup, ramekin, or another heatproof vessel. Set aside.

WHEN YOUR RICE IS TENDER and the liquid has been absorbed, pour browned butter over rice and stir to combine. Serve as soon as you can.

HOW TO COOK BASIC RICE

To cook rice of any variety (except quick-cooking rice—which is dreadful and not worth the few minutes it saves you—and sticky or creamy rice varieties used mostly for sushi and risotto), bring a ratio of 2 parts water, 1 part rice, and a pinch of salt to a boil. Cover, and then simmer for 25 minutes. When the rice is tender but still firm, and just beginning to stick to the bottom of the pot, it's perfect. The water should be completely absorbed by then, and you can fluff the rice with a fork and set it aside for several minutes.

1 CUP RICE SERVES 4

RICE AND BEANS

Variations of this side dish are common throughout Latin America and the Caribbean, served any time of day, including breakfast.

SERVES 4

1 CUP RICE (TRY BROWN BASMATI RICE OR SHORT- OR LONG-GRAIN BROWN RICE)

1 TABLESPOON UNSALTED BUTTER, PLUS EXTRA FOR SERVING

1 MEDIUM ONION, CHOPPED

SALT

1/2 CAN (7 TO 8 FL. OZ.) BLACK BEANS, PINTO BEANS, RED BEANS, OR RED KIDNEY BEANS, RINSED AND DRAINED

EXTRA-VIRGIN OLIVE OIL, TO TASTE

1 SCALLION, FINELY CHOPPED

IN A LARGE SAUCEPAN, cook rice (see instructions on page 177).

MEANWHILE, in a frying pan, melt butter. Add chopped onion and a pinch of salt, and sauté until onion is golden brown. Remove pan from heat and reserve.

FIVE MINUTES before your rice is done, gently fold beans into rice. Cover and continue cooking until rice is tender and liquid is absorbed.

TRANSFER cooked rice and beans to the pan of cooked onions, add a little more butter and a drizzle of olive oil, and gently stir to combine. Garnish with chopped scallion. Serve right from the pan or transfer to a platter.

MINTED RICE AND PEAS

This recipe only works with fresh mint. Fortunately, it grows like a weed nearly everywhere all summer long and into the fall, and is one of the sturdiest and most reliable winter imports. As for the peas, if it's summer and you can find them fresh, by all means use those, but you can use frozen peas, too.

1 CUP RICE

1/2 CUP UNSALTED BUTTER

1 SHALLOT, FINELY DICED

1 BUNCH OF FRESH MINT (RESERVE 2 WHOLE SPRIGS), LEAVES COARSELY CHOPPED

1 CUP FRESH OR FROZEN PEAS (IF FROZEN, THAWED)

SERVES 4

IN A LARGE SAUCEPAN, cook rice (see instructions on page 177).

MEANWHILE, in a pan over medium heat, melt butter until it stops bubbling. Add shallot and sauté until it softens. Muddle 1 sprig of mint by rolling it between your palms to bring out its flavourful oils, and then add to the pan. Cook for 1 more minute, then set the pan aside.

FIVE MINUTES before your rice is cooked, gently fold peas into rice. Cover pan and continue cooking until rice is tender and liquid is absorbed. Discard sprig of mint. Add minty butter and shallot mixture along with chopped mint, and gently fold to combine.

SERVE on a platter or in a nice bowl, garnished with mint leaves plucked from the remaining sprig.

TIP: Dress up this dish with a quartered hard-boiled egg.

CORN FOUR WAYS

On my way up to our family cottage, I love stopping at the farm gates along the country roads for tomatoes, blueberries, new garlic and onions, and of course sweet corn—huge stacks of freshly cut cobs piled high on the farmer's wagon, sometimes with only a collection bucket and a note listing the prices. If there is anything that tells us that summer is not only here but will one day be coming to an end, it's the appearance of sweet corn. I can usually sense a whisper of September on the breeze, so I buy much more than I need, knowing that I can slice the kernels off any cobs I can't devour before they pass their prime and freeze them. Here are four ways to take advantage of the harvest while it lasts.

GRILLED CORN
IN THE HUSK WITH CHILI AND LIME

Grilling corn in its husk seems completely natural, packaged as it is *en papillote* by Mother Nature. It pays to soak the cobs (in their husks) in water first, so the husks won't burn too much on the grill. A gimmick I like to use:peel a 1-inch-wide section of husk on one side of the cob completely down to the kernels, exposing them directly to the heat of the grill. This lets you measure the overall doneness of the corn by the colour of the kernels. Or squeeze the cob with your fingers. If it gives a little, it's cooked through.

CORN ON THE COB
UNSALTED BUTTER, MELTED (ABOUT 1/2 TABLE-
    SPOON PER COB)
LIME, QUARTERED (1/4 LIME PER COB),
    FOR ZESTING AND JUICING
CHILI POWDER (OR SEE RECIPE ON PAGE 123)
SALT

BEING CAREFUL to leave the husk attached at the base of each stalk, carefully peel down the corn husk, exposing the kernels.

IN A BOWL, combine melted butter and lime juice. Brush liberally over each cob. Sprinkle with lime zest, chili spice, and a little salt. Return the husk so it's covering each cob. Peel an inch-wide section of husk down the whole cob and remove it so that you have a strip of exposed kernels.

PREPARE YOUR CHARCOAL GRILL to peak heat (coals whitened, your hand tolerating just 2 seconds of heat when held 4 inches above the grill) or heat your gas grill to 500°F (preheated on High for 10 minutes, lid closed).

PLACE YOUR CORN on the grill and cook, turning every minute or so, until the exposed kernels are tender and darkened in spots, about 8 minutes (the husk will burn in parts, but that's okay). The corn will poach nicely inside the husk. When the corn is done, remove from heat and set aside while you grill the rest of your meal. The cobs will stay warm enough in their husk jackets for up to 30 minutes.

OPEN-GRILLED CORN ON THE COB

Grilled corn is a staple at seasonal fairs across North America. Its unmistakable aroma mingles with the smells of smoky barbecues, the diesel and dust of the midway rides, and the calls of fairground workers urging you to test your skills. The recipe is truly elemental: simply husk your cob and turn it on a hot grill until it softens and starts to colour, then slather it in butter. I feel like a kid again every time I eat it. By all means try this wonderful and basic way of grilling corn, but if you'd like to shorten your grilling time—helpful if you have other things to do on the grill—try this recipe. You can rest assured that your grilled corn will turn out perfectly cooked every time.

CORN ON THE COB, HUSKED

UNSALTED BUTTER

SALT

BRING A LARGE POT of water to a rolling boil. Add a pinch of salt for every cob, then carefully drop in the cobs. Boil for 3 minutes. Transfer the cobs to a platter and set aside.

PREPARE YOUR CHARCOAL GRILL to peak heat (coals whitened, your hand tolerating just 2 seconds of heat when held 4 inches above the grill) or heat your gas grill to 500°F (preheated on High for 10 minutes, lid closed).

PLACE YOUR CORN on the grill and cook, turning every minute or so, until browned slightly on all sides (about 4 minutes total). Transfer grilled cobs to a baking pan. Coat hot cobs with butter and a dusting of salt.

COVER WITH FOIL and set aside until the rest of your meal is ready. The cobs will stay warm enough for up to 30 minutes.

TEX-MEX ROADHOUSE CORN

Corn on the cob dressed up this way is so tasty and substantial, I've served it as an appetizer with cocktails, pre-steak—that margarita on page 58 is just perfect, for instance—and it has never failed to set the stage for the feast to come. It works equally well as a dazzling side dish, and is as messy as it is irresistible. You will be happy to have extra napkins.

CORN ON THE COB, HUSKED

PER CORN COB

1/2 DRIED ANCHO PEPPER

1/2 CUP CRÈME FRAÎCHE OR HIGH-QUALITY SOUR CREAM

SALT, TO TASTE

1/4 CUP CRUMBLED QUESO FRESCO OR COARSELY GRATED AGED CHEDDAR CHEESE

1/4 LIME

1 SCALLION, THINLY SLICED

CHILI POWDER (OR SEE RECIPE ON PAGE 123), TO TASTE

PLACE DRIED PEPPERS in a bowl and cover with warm water. Set aside for 15 minutes, until softened. Drain, remove seeds, then using a fork, mash into a paste. Add crème fraîche and stir well. Season with salt, and then set aside.

BRING A LARGE POT OF WATER to a rolling boil. Add a pinch of salt for every cob, then carefully drop in the cobs. Boil for 3 minutes. Transfer the cobs to a platter and set aside.

PREPARE YOUR CHARCOAL GRILL to peak heat (coals whitened, your hand tolerating just 2 seconds of heat when held 4 inches above the grill) or heat your gas grill to 500°F (preheated on High for 10 minutes, lid closed).

MEANWHILE, scatter your cheese over a large plate and set aside.

PLACE YOUR CORN on the grill and cook, turning every minute or so, until there is some browning on all sides, about 4 minutes total. Liberally slather ancho cream sauce on the corn, reserving some for garnish. Squeeze lime juice overtop and continue to cook, turning the saucy cobs on the grill for another minute.

REMOVE COBS from heat and roll in cheese. Serve slathered with a little more sauce, a sprinkling of scallions, and a dusting of chili powder.

CREAMY CORN

I make this a lot in the winter, with kernels I've sliced off the cob and frozen the summer before. Freezing perfectly preserves the corn, and it's pretty good cooked and served simply with a little butter and salt. It doesn't take much effort, though, to give the kernels their due, frying them with some onions and chilies, and then blanketing them in crème fraîche and a little cheddar.

SERVES 4

1 TABLESPOON UNSALTED BUTTER

1 MEDIUM ONION, DICED

1 JALAPEÑO PEPPER, THINLY SLICED

2 CUPS FRESH OR FROZEN CORN KERNELS
(IF FROZEN, THAWED AND DRAINED)

1/2 CUP CRÈME FRAÎCHE

1/2 CUP SHREDDED SHARP (OLD) CHEDDAR
CHEESE

SALT, TO TASTE

SMOKED PAPRIKA

FRESH FLAT-LEAF PARSLEY, LEAVES AND
TENDER STEMS, CHOPPED

IN A FRYING PAN over medium heat, melt butter. Add onion and sliced jalapeño, and cook until onion softens, about 2 minutes.

ADD CORN and continue cooking for 4 minutes, until the corn is tender. Reduce the heat to medium-low and stir in crème fraîche. Simmer for 1 minute, then stir in cheese. Continue cooking until cheese has melted and sauce has thickened. Season with salt.

SERVE RIGHT IN THE PAN or transfer to a bowl, dusted with a pinch of paprika and a sprinkle of parsley.

POTATOES FOUR WAYS

Complete this sentence: _____ and potatoes. If you guessed "meat," you're good. If you guessed "steak," then you already know how perfect the texture and taste of a well-cooked potato goes with a righteous steak. These potato recipes are fairly straightforward, but I've taken some extra care to let you know all the little details that I think let this humble tuber show its full splendour. For the most part, these recipes are quick, easy, or both, and act so phenomenally well in a supporting role to steak that you'll turn to them often.

ROASTED BABY POTATOES WITH HERBS

· ·

These small potatoes cook relatively quickly and can be held in the oven for up to 20 minutes before you serve them, which is pretty convenient if you happen to be cooking a steak. I think they are best when their skins have just started to wrinkle, so that they resist your bite a little before they yield their creamy, nutty flesh. Herbes de Provence seem divinely designed for the purpose of roasting baby potatoes, but you can use any mix of fine aromatic herbs. And here's a tip: Wash the potatoes but don't dry them—I find the little water that clings to the potatoes helps them turn out nicer.

15 TO 18 BABY POTATOES (ASSORTED COLOURS IF AVAILABLE)
3 TABLESPOONS OLIVE OIL (APPROX.), FOR COOKING
1/2 TEASPOON SALT
2 TABLESPOONS DRIED HERBS (SUCH AS HERBES DE PROVENCE, OR A MIX OF THYME, MARJORAM, ROSEMARY, AND SAGE) OR 1/2 CUP FRESH HERBS

SERVES 4 TO 6

· ·

PREHEAT your oven to 400°F.

ARRANGE THE POTATOES in a single layer in a heavy cast-iron, stainless-steel, or non-stick pan (with a heat-cookie bottom). Cover with oil and season with salt.

IF USING DRIED HERBS, rub between your hands and toss them onto the potatoes. If using fresh, chop finely before adding to potatoes. Toss potatoes in the pan until well coated.

ROAST in preheated oven for 30 minutes. Remove pan from oven and shake or stir it to turn the potatoes over (you don't have to be too fussy about this step, but it's good to have at least some of the potatoes cook against the metal on both sides). Return pan to oven and cook for an additional 15 minutes, or until potatoes are tender and the skins just begin to wrinkle.

YOU CAN KEEP THESE in the warm oven for 20 minutes before they start to deteriorate. After some practice, you will know to simply turn your oven off 5 minutes or so after the first 30 minutes and just leave them alone as you go about the rest of your business.

ROSEMARY AND THYME HASSELBACK POTATOES

If you have a campfire, these potatoes are fantastic individually wrapped in foil and cooked in the coals. This oven version is tasty and simple, with the butter and herbs baked right in. After you serve this comforting dish, your guests will speak well of you for years to come.

SERVES 6

12 MEDIUM POTATOES (I USE YOUNGER RED AND YELLOW POTATOES, BUT ANY WILL DO JUST FINE)
1 CUP UNSALTED BUTTER, MELTED
1 BUNCH EACH OF FRESH ROSEMARY AND THYME (RESERVE A FEW SPRIGS TO GARNISH)
SALT AND PEPPER

PREHEAT your oven to 400°F.

USING A SHARP KNIFE, carefully cut each potato into thin slices, leaving 1/4 inch at the bottom intact (be careful not to cut the potatoes all the way through). Transfer to a baking sheet.

ROAST in preheated oven for 30 to 40 minutes, then test: Squeeze a potato gently from the sides. If the slits you've cut widen under the pressure but the potato is otherwise still firm, you're ready for the next step. If not, return pan to the hot oven for another 7 to 10 minutes, and then check again.

WHEN THE SLITS in the potatoes widen when squeezed, brush each potato generously with butter and insert sprigs of thyme and rosemary where you can into the slits. Sprinkle more herbs all over, and season liberally with salt. Roast for another 15 to 25 minutes, until the potatoes are as tender as you like, their skins wrinkly from the bake, and the herbs have noticeably dried. Sprinkle with salt, to taste, and a few grinds of pepper.

TO SERVE, garnish with the remaining fresh herbs, for colour and emphasis.

CLASSIC POTATO PANCAKES

The potato rösti, latke, and pancake are all variations on the same theme. The difference generally comes down to the amount of egg and flour in the mix. I've grown fond of the proportions here because they work so well every time. They are also easy to remember: 4 potatoes, 4 tablespoons flour, 2 eggs. The rest of the ingredients, though important, add flavour and texture. If you can remember the first three ingredients, you have the basics to be as creative as you like. A note on the frying fat: I much prefer animal fats to vegetable fats for cooking, especially with high-temperature cooking. This old-school way of frying tastes so much better, is better for you (because saturated fats are much more stable when heated), and, I think, performs better, especially as we are looking for colour and crisp textures in this recipe in particular.

4 LARGE POTATOES, COARSELY GRATED
1 MEDIUM ONION, COARSELY GRATED
4 TABLESPOONS ALL-PURPOSE FLOUR
2 LARGE EGGS, LIGHTLY BEATEN
1/2 TEASPOON SALT
FRESHLY GROUND BLACK PEPPER
DUCK FAT OR LARD, TALLOW, OR OTHER
   HIGH-QUALITY ANIMAL FAT (GRAPESEED OR
   CANOLA OIL IN A PINCH)
CRÈME FRAÎCHE OR SOUR CREAM, FOR SERVING

MAKES 4 TO 6 PANCAKES

IN A MIXING BOWL, combine potatoes and onion. Using your hands, squeeze out the juice (do this over a fine-mesh sieve or wrap the mixture in a kitchen towel, roll up, and squeeze). Return mixture to bowl and let sit for 10 minutes, then wring it out again (the fry will turn out better if there is less water in the mixture).

TO THE POTATOES, add flour, eggs, salt, and a couple of grinds of pepper. Stir until well combined. Set aside.

HEAT about 1/4 inch of fat in a heavy frying pan (cast iron or stainless steel work well, or a non-stick pan with a heat-cookie bottom) over medium-high heat, until the fat begins to shimmer. Carefully place a ball of the potato mixture into the pan (about a heaping 1/4 cup), and then, using a spatula, flatten until about 1/2 inch thick. Cook pancakes in batches, being careful not to overcrowd the pan, for 4 to 5 minutes per side, until they are golden brown with a crispy crust. Transfer to a plate lined in paper towel and keep in a warm oven or just at room temperature until all the batter is used up. (You may have to add more fat to the pan.)

SERVE with a little crème fraîche.

SMASHED FRIED POTATOES

The brute physics of this dish is a marvel of simplicity. Three straightforward steps: cook, smash, fry (and enjoy!).

AS MANY MEDIUM POTATOES AS YOU HAVE GUESTS, INDIVIDUALLY WRAPPED IN FOIL FOR BAKING (SEE TIP)

1 TABLESPOON COOKING FAT OF YOUR CHOICE (LARD, TALLOW, OR DUCK FAT)

2 SPRIGS FRESH THYME PER POTATO

CRÈME FRAÎCHE, FOR SERVING

PREHEAT your oven to 400°F.

PLACE WRAPPED POTATOES on a baking sheet and bake in preheated oven for 45 minutes, or until tender (they should yield with a little squeeze; if not, continue baking until they do, another 10 minutes or so). When they are done, carefully remove pan from the oven, unwrap each potato, and let cool for 10 minutes.

USING YOUR PALM (insulated by a kitchen towel if potatoes are still hot) or a spatula, gently flatten each potato until it is as flat as it can get without falling apart, about 1 inch thick. For the first potato, flatten gradually to test its tolerance. If it hasn't cooled enough it will indeed fall apart. You can do this part in advance, but don't wait hours before you flatten the potato because the proteins and starches will have recongealed, and the potato will have become a bit gluey and more brittle.

IN A HEAVY CAST-IRON, stainless-steel, or non-stick pan (with a heat-cookie bottom) over medium-high heat, melt your fat of choice. Place a sprig of thyme in the pan, and then a flattened potato on top. Fry for 4 minutes, then turn the potato over, putting a fresh sprig of thyme underneath, and fry for another 3 to 4 minutes. When done, the potato's skin should be crisp and browned, and the thyme darkened.

SERVE IMMEDIATELY, with a little crème fraîche and the sprigs of toasted thyme on top.

TIP: As a speedy alternative to baking potatoes, place them—unwrapped—in the microwave and cook on High for 5 to 6 minutes per potato.

FAST AND DELICIOUS REFRIED BEANS

Making refried beans from dried beans is admirable, but I admit I use canned beans quite a lot, which of course is much faster. The tasty, murky liquid left over in from-scratch recipes (the "sopa") is used to emulsify the smashed beans into a paste. In this recipe, I use beef, chicken, or vegetable stock, because I find the liquid left in canned beans to be gluey and sometimes very salty. Refried beans are quite versatile, and there have been weeks where I've used them easily as much as mashed potatoes. You may just fall in love with them. When I fry up high-quality bacon, I save the rendered fat specially to make this dish.

2 TABLESPOONS LARD, TALLOW, RENDERED BACON FAT, SCHMALTZ, OR OTHER FAT OF YOUR CHOICE

1 MEDIUM ONION, DICED

1 CAN (15 FL. OZ) PINTO, BLACK, OR RED KIDNEY BEANS, RINSED AND DRAINED

1 CUP BEEF, CHICKEN, OR VEGETABLE STOCK, PLUS MORE FOR THINNING, IF NEEDED

SALT, TO TASTE

QUESO FRESCO OR FETA, FOR CRUMBLING

SERVES 4

IN A CAST-IRON, stainless-steel, or non-stick frying pan (with a heat-cookie bottom) over medium-high heat, heat fat. Fry diced onion until it becomes translucent and golden brown at the edges, 4 to 5 minutes.

ADD BEANS and cook for 2 minutes, stirring from time to time. Stir in 1 cup stock. Using a potato masher or wooden spoon, mash beans and stock into a chunky paste. Reduce the heat to medium-low and continue cooking until you like the consistency. If the paste becomes too thick, just stir in more stock to thin it out. Season with salt to taste.

SERVE refried beans alongside just about anything. It's particularly good with a little queso fresco or feta crumbled on top.

PAN-ROASTED SQUASH AND ONIONS

Squash can seem intimidating, but once you get over opening up the fruit, it's a cinch to cook. Cutting open a squash takes a little care. Make sure your hands are dry, your cutting surface is stable, and that you are using a chef's knife. For most medium-size squashes, skewer the squash straight through the side, and then carefully lever the knife down through the fruit until the squash falls in half. If it moves around too much because of its shape, slice a small bit off the side to flatten it enough so that it stays put while you open it. This initial fuss is worth it. I love the autumnal, nutty, toasty taste of squash. This recipe is dead easy, immensely satisfying as a side dish to just about anything, and perfect for steak dinners, since it practically cooks itself while you cook your steak. I've used a hubbard squash here, but nearly any winter squash will do. Don't even think of peeling it—the skin is thin, most of the time, and will soften up nicely when it's roasted.

1 MEDIUM WINTER SQUASH (SMALLER HUBBARDS, ACORN, AND BUTTERNUT WORK WELL), CUT INTO 2-INCH CHUNKS

1 MEDIUM ONION, CUT INTO 8 WEDGES (ROOT END TRIMMED BUT INTACT, TO HOLD IT TOGETHER)

4 CLOVES GARLIC

1 TABLESPOON OLIVE OIL, FOR COOKING

PINCH OF SALT

FRESHLY GROUND BLACK PEPPER

FRESHLY GRATED PARMESAN CHEESE, FOR SERVING

SERVES 4

PREHEAT your oven to 375°F.

IN A LARGE CAST-IRON PAN or baking sheet, arrange squash in a single layer (be careful not to overcrowd the pan; any unused, cut squash can be stored raw in the fridge for a week).

ADD the onion, garlic, olive oil, salt, and a few grinds of pepper. Toss to coat.

ROAST in preheated oven for 35 minutes, then check for doneness: squash should be soft and beginning to darken at the edges; onions and garlic should be caramelized and golden brown. If this is not the case, continue roasting for another 5 to 6 minutes and check again.

TRANSFER roasted vegetables to a bowl and serve. If you want to kick up the savoury and nutty flavours, sprinkle with a little finely grated Parmesan.

GRILLED WHOLE PLANTAIN

Plantains, if you aren't already familiar with them, are very easy-going fruit, as happy in a savoury setting as they are in a sweet one. Inexpensive, uncomplicated, and pretty much available anywhere you find their banana cousins, they will surprise and delight your guests nonetheless. Perhaps the simplest recipe in this book, grilled plantains take just minutes to cook and require almost zero prep time. Because you grill the plantains right in their skins, they stay warm long after they are removed from the heat, their terrifically nutty, savoury-sweet flesh no worse for wear. Plenty of butter and crème fraîche or sour cream is key. I've also dressed these with grilled chilies, onions, and peppers, but you can load up a grilled plantain just as you might a baked potato: crispy bacon, chopped scallions, shredded cheddar, refried beans, diced tomato. The possibilities are nearly endless.

AS MANY RIPE PLANTAINS AS YOU LIKE, UNPEELED (SEE TIP)

PER PLANTAIN
JALAPEÑO PEPPER, RED CHILI, OR HOT PEPPER OF YOUR CHOICE, OR TO TASTE (GRILL WHOLE)
1/4 BELL PEPPER (ANY COLOUR), THINLY SLICED
1/2 MEDIUM ONION, THINLY SLICED INTO RINGS
1 TABLESPOON UNSALTED BUTTER
SALT, TO TASTE
1 TABLESPOON CRÈME FRAÎCHE OR SOUR CREAM

PREPARE YOUR CHARCOAL GRILL to one-third cooler than peak heat, or heat your gas grill to medium-high (preheated on High for 10 minutes, lid closed).

USING THE POINT OF A SHARP KNIFE, poke a small hole in the middle of the fruit, piercing the skin down to the flesh. Place plantain on grill, along with hot peppers and onion. Cook plantain, flipping once or twice to ensure even cooking, until completely blackened, 5 to 6 minutes (it should feel softer when squeezed, and quite hot all the way through when checked with a small incision). Your sliced onion and peppers should be softened and browned, and ready about the same time, perhaps earlier; be prepared to transfer them to a plate and keep warm while the plantain finishes cooking. (Grilled plantain can also be set aside in a warm oven or on a warm grill for up to 30 minutes if needed.) Slice and deseed hot peppers before serving.

TO SERVE, cut grilled plantain open lengthwise and top with butter and salt, a dollop of crème fraîche, and the grilled peppers and onion. Serve immediately.

TIP: When buying plantain for this recipe, look for skins that are at least as black as they are yellow, or even more so. This means that their flesh will be soft and sweet.

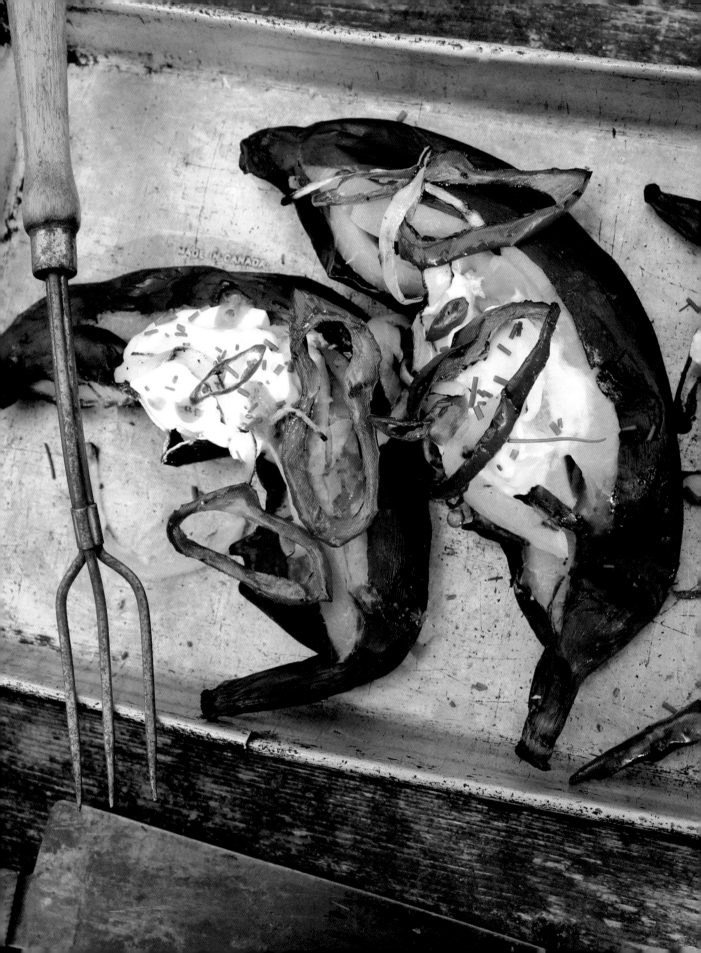

SAVOURY PLANTAIN PANCAKES

Living up to the plantain's easy-going reputation, this recipe is fast and simple, but manages to pack in a lot of satisfying flavour and texture. It makes a tasty side to a great steak for dinner, or served with eggs for breakfast. It's easy to remember, too: just use 1 plantain, 1 egg, and 1 tablespoon of flour for the pancake, and the rest is up to you. I've suggested some other flavourings here to inspire you.

MAKES 2 PANCAKES

1 RIPE PLANTAIN, PEELED (SEE TIP)
1 EGG, BEATEN
1 TABLESPOON ALL-PURPOSE FLOUR, PLUS EXTRA AS NEEDED
1/4 TEASPOON SALT
1/2 MEDIUM ONION, COARSELY GRATED
1/4 TEASPOON GROUND NUTMEG
FAT OR OIL, FOR FRYING (EQUAL PARTS BUTTER AND OLIVE OIL WORK WELL HERE, AS DOES LARD OR DUCK FAT)
CRÈME FRAÎCHE, SOUR CREAM, OR YOGURT, FOR SERVING

IN A BOWL, using your hands or a potato masher, smash plantain. Add beaten egg, flour, and salt. Stir well, then add grated onion and nutmeg; stir to combine. The batter should resemble a thin porridge. If it's too thin, add a little more flour.

IN A FRYING PAN over medium-high heat, heat fat until it begins to shimmer. Pour in half of the plantain batter (reserve the rest) and cook pancake until the edges darken at the bottom and some bubbling appears on top, 2 to 3 minutes. Flip over and cook bottom until golden brown. Transfer pancake to a plate, keeping warm. Repeat with remaining batter, adding more fat or oil to the pan if necessary.

SERVE IMMEDIATELY with your choice of topping.

TIP: When buying plantain for this recipe, look for skins that are at least as black as they are yellow, or even more so. This means that their flesh will be soft and sweet.

SALADS

WHEN I THINK OF SUMMER, I DREAM OF GRILLED BAVETTE STEAKS, MADE BETTER ALONGSIDE A BRILLIANTLY RIPE AND SULTRY TOMATO SALAD WITH SUMMER HERBS. WHEN I'M COZY IN THE DARK OF WINTER, I DREAM OF RIB STEAK: RICH AND IMPOSSIBLY GOOD BESIDE ROASTED PARSNIPS AND POTATOES. HERE ARE STEAK-FRIENDLY SALADS FOR EVERY SEASON, AND SOME CLASSICS THAT ARE TERRIFIC ALL YEAR LONG.

GRAPES AND WINTER GREENS WITH HONEY DIJON MUSTARD

In the dead of winter, most salad greens just aren't the same as they are at other times of year. Some hold up remarkably well, though: endive, escarole, and radicchios like treviso and chioggia. They tend to be on the bitter side, which is why the dressing for this salad is a bit sweeter and thicker, and the winter greens are joined by romaine and the juicy surprise of red grapes. You will notice that there is some knife work here, helping to balance the mouthfeel and appearance.

SERVES 4 TO 6

1/2 HEAD ROMAINE LETTUCE, CUT LENGTHWISE TWICE, THEN EACH LENGTH CUT INTO 1-INCH PIECES

2 ENDIVES, CUT LENGTHWISE, THEN EACH LENGTH CUT INTO 1/2-INCH PIECES

1 HEAD TREVISO, CUT LENGTHWISE TWICE, THEN EACH LENGTH CUT INTO 1/2-INCH PIECES

1 BUNCH OF FRESH MINT, LEAVES ONLY

1/2 BUNCH OF SEEDLESS RED GRAPES (ABOUT 20), HALVED LENGTHWISE

5 TABLESPOONS EXTRA-VIRGIN OLIVE OIL

2 TABLESPOONS WHITE WINE VINEGAR

PINCH OF SALT

1 TABLESPOON DIJON MUSTARD

1 TEASPOON LIQUID HONEY

FRESHLY GROUND BLACK PEPPER

PLACE all of the greens, including the mint, in a big salad bowl. Add grapes. Set aside.

IN A JAR OR CUP, combine olive oil, vinegar, and salt. Shake or whisk to dissolve the salt in the vinegar, then add mustard and honey. Taste and adjust honey and vinegar as you like, with a bias toward sweetness.

TO SERVE the salad, add two-thirds of the dressing to the salad and toss to coat. Reserve remaining dressing to serve on the side, for those who want more. Finish with a little pepper on top.

BIG CROUTON YOGURT CAESAR SALAD

This salad will remind you of an actual Caesar, but since it doesn't have anchovies or raw egg yolks, that's as far as it goes. Still, the garlicky yogurt and mustard inform a heady, creamy dressing that would make Brutus double take. When it comes to the bacon, you might as well buy the best you can find, since it's only a small amount. I use pancetta here, which I think really stands out in an already very tasty salad.

SERVES 4 TO 6

1/2 POUND PANCETTA OR GOOD THICK-CUT
    SMOKY BACON, CUT INTO 1/8-INCH SQUARES
1/4 WHOLE-WHEAT PLOWMAN'S LOAF (OR ANY
    SOFT LOAF), CUT INTO 1-INCH CUBES
SALT
SWEET PAPRIKA
1 HEAD ROMAINE LETTUCE, TRIMMED AND CUT
    INTO 2-INCH PIECES, WASHED AND WELL DRIED
1 TABLESPOON PLAIN FULL-FAT (10% OR HIGHER)
    GREEK YOGURT
1 TABLESPOON WELL-CRUMBLED FETA CHEESE
    PLUS 1 TEASPOON FETA BRINE (OPTIONAL)
4 TABLESPOONS EXTRA-VIRGIN OLIVE OIL,
    PLUS MORE FOR CROUTONS
4 TEASPOONS WHITE BALSAMIC VINEGAR OR
    WHITE WINE VINEGAR (IF USING THE LATTER,
    ADD DRIZZLE OF LIQUID HONEY)
1 TEASPOON DIJON MUSTARD
1 LARGE CLOVE GARLIC, OR 2 SMALLER CLOVES,
    MINCED
FRESHLY GRATED PARMESAN CHEESE,
    FOR SERVING
1/2 LEMON CUT INTO WEDGES

PREHEAT your oven to 400°F.

IN A FRYING PAN over medium heat, fry pancetta until crispy and crunchy. Transfer to a plate lined in paper towel and set aside.

SPREAD bread cubes evenly over a baking sheet and drizzle with olive oil. Sprinkle with salt. Toss until evenly coated, then dust lightly with paprika. Bake in preheated oven for 10 minutes, or until just toasted on the outside and getting harder on the inside but not completely dried out. Remove pan from oven and set aside, uncovered.

PLACE LETTUCE in a large bowl and set aside.

IN A JAR OR BOWL, combine yogurt, feta and its brine (if using), olive oil, vinegar, honey (if using), mustard, and minced garlic. Shake or whisk until creamy. Taste and adjust as you see fit.

TO SERVE, toss dressing and pancetta with lettuce until the leaves are well coated. Drop in croutons and finish with finely grated Parmesan and lemon wedges.

ARUGULA AND PINE NUTS
WITH WARM BACON DRESSING

I love putting this salad together partly because it is properly decadent, partly because the smell of roasting nuts puts a smile on my face, and partly because I get to cook bacon and then use the fat. The dressing works so well with arugula, which turns out perfectly with just a tiny bit of wilting from the warmth of the pan. It's a total cinch, too, and will warm your heart while making you feel more powerful than you thought possible from a salad. I like to use sweet rice vinegar here because it is a little sweeter and generally a bit less acidic than others. It's a great vinegar to have in your cupboard.

SERVES 4 TO 6

1/4 CUP PINE NUTS

4 STRIPS NICE BACON

1/2 TABLESPOON SWEET RICE VINEGAR (OR WHITE BALSAMIC VINEGAR OR WHITE WINE VINEGAR WITH A LITTLE SUGAR, TO TASTE)

5 TO 6 CUPS LOOSELY PACKED YOUNG ARUGULA

IN A DRY HEAVY CAST-IRON, stainless-steel, or non-stick pan (with a heat-cookie bottom) over medium heat, toast the pine nuts until they start to brown, shaking the pan to turn them. Be watchful: at first nothing will happen, but then they can darken very quickly. When they are nicely golden brown, remove pan from heat and transfer toasted pine nuts to a ramekin or small bowl.

IN THE SAME PAN, fry bacon until crisp. Transfer to a plate lined in paper towel, reserving the fat in the pan.

LET PAN COOL for 10 to 15 minutes, until you can touch the bacon fat with your finger for 2 or 3 seconds without discomfort. Add vinegar. Taste and adjust with more if you like (if you've added too much, adjust with a little olive oil). The bacon fat should still be in liquid form at this point, but if it has begun to solidify, warm it briefly over low heat (then turn off the heat). To the pan, add arugula and gently toss to coat the leaves.

SERVE in a large salad bowl or on individual serving plates, with crumbled bacon and toasted pine nuts on top.

ROASTED TANGY ROOT BOWL

This is definitely a wintery dish. It is best served warm, and is substantial enough that I often make it for my wife (who is vegetarian, if you can believe it) as a stand-alone meal, with a little feta cheese crumbled on top. You can use different roots (and bulbs and tubers), but I find this combination works really well, and looks beautiful.

SERVES 4 TO 6

2 MEDIUM PURPLE ONIONS

2 MEDIUM CARROTS

2 MEDIUM PARSNIPS

2 EACH MEDIUM RED AND YELLOW BEETS

2 MEDIUM YELLOW POTATOES

EXTRA-VIRGIN OLIVE OIL

ANY SWEET VINEGAR (BALSAMIC, WHITE BALSAMIC, OR RICE VINEGAR)

SALT AND PEPPER

PREHEAT your oven to 400°F.

CUT ONIONS into 8 wedges, leaving enough of the root end intact to keep the onion layers connected. Cut carrots and parsnips widthwise into 2- to 3-inch pieces, then halve lengthwise. Cut beets and potatoes into 8 wedges each.

SPREAD CUT VEGETABLES evenly over a baking sheet. Drizzle liberally with olive oil, then sprinkle with vinegar and a dusting of salt and pepper. Using your hands, toss the vegetables until well coated. Roast in preheated oven for 30 minutes, or until vegetables are tender, starting to shrink and darken, and somewhat sticky from the caramelizing vinegar. If they're not, keep roasting and checking every 6 to 8 minutes.

SERVE hot or warm.

MONSTER GREEK SALAD

Feta, olives, and oregano make this salad "Greek." Octopus turns it into something that will bring out your inner kraken. You can skip the octopus if you like, and you will still have a wonderfully balanced salad. It is best crisp and fresh, so save the dressing and tossing until the last second before serving. If you're serving it plated, you can hold back some of the feta, olives, and octopus, and place those more expressly on the greens to make it picture perfect.

1 HEAD ROMAINE LETTUCE

1 ENGLISH CUCUMBER, THINLY SLICED

1 LARGE RED BELL PEPPER, THINLY SLICED

1 RED ONION, HALVED AND THINLY SLICED

4 OUNCES GOOD-QUALITY FETA CHEESE, CRUMBLED INTO CHUNKS

1/2 POUND COOKED, MARINATED OCTOPUS (FROM THE DELI COUNTER), CUT INTO BITES

1 BUNCH OF FRESH MINT, LEAVES ONLY

10 TO 12 KALAMATA OLIVES (FROM THE DELI COUNTER, PITS AND ALL)

5 TABLESPOONS EXTRA-VIRGIN OLIVE OIL

2 TABLESPOONS WHITE BALSAMIC VINEGAR OR WHITE WINE VINEGAR

1 TABLESPOON DRIED OREGANO (GREEK MOUNTAIN OREGANO FLORETS ARE BEST, BUT DRIED LEAVES ARE OKAY)

SERVES 4 TO 6

GENTLY TEAR the nicest leaves of your romaine into bite-size pieces (include the juicy, tender, very palatable stalks) into a big salad bowl. Add sliced cucumber, bell pepper, onion, feta, octopus, mint, and olives, in that order (do this purposefully so it looks attractive before you toss in the dressing at the table). Set aside.

IN A JAR OR CUP, combine olive oil and vinegar. Shake or whisk, then taste, adjusting with more vinegar as necessary.

TO SERVE the salad, add two-thirds of the dressing to the salad and toss to coat. Reserve remaining dressing to serve on the side, for those who want more. Then (and only then) rub dried oregano firmly between your hands and sprinkle over the salad (it's much better this way, otherwise it becomes rather soggy from the dressing).

REAWAKEN YOUR LETTUCE

If you find that your lettuce has wilted in the fridge, there is a way to bring it back. Simply break off the leaves close to the bottom of the stalk (and discard that part) and submerge in a bowl of cool water. Wait 15 to 20 minutes, and behold: the lettuce will be turgid and practically climbing out of the bowl. This also works for lettuce that may seem good enough for your ham sandwich but that you want extra crisp for a nice salad. Another thing: make sure your lettuce is truly dry before you dress it. Droplets of water on your greens will repel and dilute the dressing, which won't be able to adhere to the leaves. Leaves coated in your terrific dressing will make you happier.

BELL PEPPER CHOP-CHOP

This chunky, crunchy, juicy salad can be made up to an hour in advance, dressed and all. The sweet, crunchy gush of bell peppers is accompanied by soft, savoury artichoke and palm hearts, and the salty kiss of Kalamata olives and feta cheese.

SERVES 4 TO 6

1 EACH LARGE YELLOW AND RED BELL PEPPER, CUT INTO 1/2-INCH SQUARES
1 MEDIUM PURPLE ONION, DICED
1/2 ENGLISH CUCUMBER, CUT IN A 1/4-INCH DICE
1 JAR (14 OUNCES) ARTICHOKE HEARTS OR PALM HEARTS, CUT INTO BITE-SIZE PIECES
4 TABLESPOONS EXTRA-VIRGIN OLIVE OIL
4 TEASPOONS ANY SWEET, PALE VINEGAR (LIKE RICE VINEGAR OR WHITE BALSAMIC VINEGAR)
12 KALAMATA OLIVES (APPROX.)
4 OUNCES FETA CHEESE
A HANDFUL OF CHOPPED FRESH FLAT-LEAF PARSLEY LEAVES AND TENDER STEMS
SALT AND PEPPER

IN A LARGE SALAD BOWL, combine all of the prepared vegetables. Drizzle with oil and vinegar (a ratio of a little more than 3:1 oil to vinegar). Top with most of the olives, and toss until well combined.

CRUMBLE OVER feta, sprinkle over parsley, and nestle any remaining olives on top. Season with salt and pepper to taste, keeping in mind that the feta is already pretty salty.

SERVE IMMEDIATELY or wait for up to 1 hour if you need to.

SUMMER TOMATO SALAD WITH HERBS GALORE

Every year between late July and late September an astounding variety of ripe and ready tomatoes become available just about everywhere. It's easy enough to find many sorts of fabulous heirloom tomatoes: green zebras, costoluto Genovese, ananas noire, old Germans, black krim, and still more. (If you want to knock yourself out with a complete list, take a look at Gail Harland's and Sofia Larrinua-Craxton's adorable and informative *Tomato: A Guide to the Pleasures of Choosing, Growing, and Cooking*, published by Dorling Kindersley in 2009). Local cherry tomatoes and regular field tomatoes are also really, really good when they are summer-ripened. So, the tomato gets top billing in this salad, with summer herbs playing an important supporting role. (If you really want to let someone know you love them, serve this topped with a little buffalo mozzarella or burrata.)

SERVES 4 TO 6

ABOUT 2 POUNDS RIPE TOMATOES (ANY SIZE, COLOUR, AND SHAPE), HALVED OR CUT INTO BITE-SIZE WEDGES
PINCH OF SALT
4 TABLESPOONS EXTRA-VIRGIN OLIVE OIL
4 TEASPOONS ANY SWEET, PALE VINEGAR (LIKE RICE VINEGAR OR WHITE BALSAMIC)
1 CLOVE GARLIC, MINCED
3 OR 4 SPRIGS EACH FRESH MINT, BASIL, AND THYME OR OTHER TENDER SUMMER HERBS, LEAVES ONLY
A HANDFUL OF FRESH CHIVES, CHOPPED
FRESHLY GROUND BLACK PEPPER

ARRANGE TOMATOES nicely in a big salad bowl. Sprinkle with salt. Set aside.

IN A JAR OR CUP, combine oil, vinegar, and garlic. Shake well or whisk to combine. Drizzle over tomatoes but don't toss. Set aside at room temperature until ready to serve.

TO SERVE, top with herbs and a few grinds of pepper and gently toss to combine.

ULTIMATE POTATO SALAD WITH FRESH GREEN PEAS

The best potato salads I've had, whatever their style, have always been made with waxy, as opposed to starchy, potatoes. Look for any baby potato, fingerling, or smooth-skinned potato. This fantastically satisfying accompaniment to steak should taste fresh and fulsome, spilling off the serving spoon easily in a coating of slightly tangy cream.

SERVES 4 TO 6

3 POUNDS BABY POTATOES OR ANY SMOOTH-SKINNED WAXY POTATO, LEFT WHOLE, SKIN ON
1/2 TABLESPOON SALT, PLUS MORE TO TASTE
4 TABLESPOONS EXTRA-VIRGIN OLIVE OIL
1 TABLESPOON SWEET, PALE VINEGAR (LIKE WHITE BALSAMIC OR RICE VINEGAR)
1 TABLESPOON GRAINY DIJON-STYLE MUSTARD
2 HEAPING TABLESPOONS CRÈME FRAÎCHE
1 CUP FRESH OR FROZEN GREEN PEAS (THAWED IF FROZEN)
1/2 BUNCH EACH OF FRESH MINT AND DILL, CHOPPED
1 SCALLION, THINLY SLICED
FRESHLY GROUND BLACK PEPPER

BOIL POTATOES in a large pot of water with 1/2 tablespoon of salt until just fork-tender. Test after 20 minutes: you are looking for a tender potato that will be firm enough to neatly cut, once cooled, without breaking. Drain and let cool in the pot as you prepare your dressing.

IN A JAR WITH A LID, combine olive oil, vinegar, and mustard. Shake well to combine. Add crème fraîche and shake vigorously until it forms something resembling loose mayonnaise. Add salt, to taste. Set aside.

BRING A SMALL POT OF WATER to a boil. Add peas and boil (blanch) for 25 seconds. Immediately transfer to a fine-mesh sieve and rinse under cold water to stop the cooking. Set aside.

CUT COOLED POTATOES into bite-size pieces, being careful to keep the skins from coming off (but don't sweat it if some do).

IN A BIG SALAD BOWL, using your hands, gently combine dressing, peas, potatoes, and herbs, reserving a few sprigs of herbs for garnish. Season to taste, and then finish with a few of the nicer leaves of mint and dill on top, along with the scallions.

SERVE while still warm or at room temperature.

DESSERTS

HERE ARE THREE DESSERTS I TURN TO CONSTANTLY. THEY AREN'T HARD TO MAKE, WHICH MEANS YOU CAN MOSTLY RELAX WHILE YOU REMINISCE ABOUT THE UNBELIEVABLE STEAK DINNER YOU'VE JUST ENJOYED. THEY ARE ALSO CLOSER TO THE LIGHTER SIDE, IF NOT ALTOGETHER LIGHT (BECAUSE WHAT WOULD THE POINT OF THAT BE?), SO YOU CAN DELIVER SATISFACTION WITHOUT OVERSTUFFING YOUR DINNER COMPANIONS.

BAKED APPLES WITH EGGY CUSTARD

Baked apples and custard is literally the first dessert I can remember my mother making for me and my brother, so many years ago. It smacks of late autumn, and I find that it is such a fine thing with a little snifter of Calvados after a nice steak dinner. Baking spices enhance the taste and aroma of apples, and this eggy custard pulls it all together. You can make the apple and custard components at the same time, or you can make either in advance, reserving the custard (covered) over a pan of hot water or in a double boiler and the baked apples in a warm oven.

BAKED APPLES

4 MEDIUM BAKING APPLES (MCINTOSH OR
   GALA WORK WELL)
1/4 CUP OLD-FASHIONED ROLLED OATS
1/4 CUP RAISINS
4 TABLESPOONS UNSALTED BUTTER, MELTED
4 TABLESPOONS LIQUID HONEY
1/4 TEASPOON EACH GROUND NUTMEG,
   CINNAMON, AND ALLSPICE, PLUS EXTRA
   FOR GARNISH

EGGY CUSTARD

2 CUPS WHOLE MILK
SEEDS FROM 1 VANILLA BEAN POD OR
   3/4 TEASPOON PURE VANILLA EXTRACT
4 EGG YOLKS
1 TABLESPOON WATER
1/4 CUP GRANULATED SUGAR
2 TEASPOONS CORNSTARCH
PINCH OF SALT

SERVES 4

MAKE THE APPLES: Preheat your oven to 375°F.

USING AN APPLE CORER, melon baller, or paring knife and a teaspoon, partially core the apples (but don't peel) from the top until you are just 1/4 inch or so from the bottom, creating a vessel that you can fill with oats and raisins.

IN A BOWL, combine oats, raisins, melted butter, honey, and spices. Stuff cored apples with this mixture.

ARRANGE STUFFED APPLES in a baking pan and bake in preheated oven for 45 minutes, or until the apples are tender and a bit sunken. Remove pan from the oven and set aside. (You can keep them in the still-warm oven if you need to set them aside for more than a few minutes.)

MAKE THE EGGY CUSTARD: In a saucepan over medium heat, combine milk and vanilla. Heat until milk just begins to froth and larger bubbles begin to appear along the sides of the pan. Remove pan from the heat and set aside.

IN A HEATPROOF MIXING BOWL, whisk together egg yolks and water until frothy. Whisk in sugar, followed by the cornstarch and a pinch of salt. Add half of the hot milk from the saucepan and whisk until smooth. Pour the eggy mixture into the saucepan with the remaining hot milk

PUT THE SAUCEPAN over medium-low heat and cook the custard, stirring with a wooden spoon or spatula, lightly dragging the bottom of the pan to keep the custard from clotting too much, until it thickens, about 20 minutes. Remove pan from the heat.

SERVE warm baked apples with eggy custard poured overtop, enough that it spills over the sides and pools on the plate. Dust with a little nutmeg, cinnamon, allspice, or all three.

TIP: Apple pairs well with many flavours, so customize your garnishes and make this dessert your own. Smashed dark chocolate goes well (as shown), as do blackberries or cranberries.

FRIED PLANTAIN,
TOASTED COCONUT, AND ICE CREAM

If you haven't tried plantain, this will be a delicious surprise (for a fantastic savoury side dish, see the recipe for grilled plantain on page 200). Plantain is not nearly as sweet as banana, and is more substantial. When fried, it caramelizes readily and holds together pretty well. Buy plantains when the peel is as much black as yellow. Or if you are using green plantains for another type of cooking, let one ripen to half-blackness or even three-quarters. Your guests will ask, "Hey, is this banana?" and you can set them straight, appearing kind and worldly, as they begin to notice the somewhat pancake-like taste and texture.

1 RIPE PLANTAIN

1 TABLESPOON UNSWEETENED SHREDDED COCONUT

4 TO 5 HAZELNUTS, COARSELY CHOPPED

1 TABLESPOON UNSALTED BUTTER

VANILLA ICE CREAM (AS MUCH AS YOU LIKE)

LIQUID HONEY, FOR DRIZZLING

FRESHLY GROUND NUTMEG, FOR DUSTING

SERVES 3 TO 4

PEEL YOUR PLANTAIN, and then cut it in half across the middle. Slice each half in thirds to get a total of six 1/4-inch strips. (You may find that your plantain is already the right size after one cut.) Set aside.

IN A DRY FRYING PAN over medium-high heat, toast coconut until golden brown, 1 to 2 minutes. Watch it carefully because at some point it will begin to darken very quickly. Remove pan from the heat, transfer the toasted coconut to a bowl, and set aside.

IN THE SAME PAN, toast the hazelnuts until they just start to brown, about 2 minutes. Remove and set aside.

IN THE SAME PAN, melt butter. Add plantain and cook until both sides are golden brown, about 2 minutes per side. Transfer cooked plantain to a plate lined in paper towel.

SERVE 1 or 2 pieces of plantain topped with a scoop of vanilla ice cream, a drizzle of honey, a scattering of hazelnuts, and a sprinkle of the toasted coconut. Finish with a light dusting of nutmeg.

CRÈME FRAÎCHE

By now you've come across crème fraîche in more than one recipe in this book. It happens to be awesome—a sweet culture that is, essentially, very rich and creamy sour cream. It is available at better food stores, but I use it often enough in sauces and on its own that I make it from scratch on a weekly basis. As it turns out, it's really easy to do. Homemade crème fraîche is also tastier, and you can control the thickness and consistency by how long you let the culture grow.

To get your first batch going, put 4 heaping tablespoons of cultured organic buttermilk in a 32-oz (1L) mason jar. Fill the rest of the jar with 35% (or higher) organic cream. You might get lucky with non-organic cream, but so many regular brands have been too adulterated with emulsifying gums, filtration, and reassembly processes that the crème fraîche culture won't develop properly. Same goes for the buttermilk. I'm not sure what commercial buttermilk is made from, but it often isn't buttermilk (be wary of labels that say "buttermilk flavour"). You need the genuine article here: the milky liquid that is left over from churning cultured butter, which is inoculated with specific bacteria.

Stir to combine. Wipe the rim of the jar with a clean cloth or paper towel, and then cover it with cheese cloth or muslin, using the mason ring to secure the cloth. Let it sit at room temperature, out of direct sunlight, for 48 hours, until it's thickened to a spreadable consistency. If it hasn't, leave it alone a few more hours (and up to a day longer), or not, depending on how thick you like it. Cover it with the snap lid and refrigerate. The culture will stop growing once refrigerated.

When you begin to run low on your crème fraîche, simply grow another batch using 4 or 5 heaping tablespoons of what you have left in a clean jar. A fresh batch should last at least a week in the fridge without changing. I've taken mine past two weeks, but as a rule I change it and start a new batch every 7 to 8 days.

Your sauces and soups will thank you. Your pasta will thank you. Your sandwiches will thank you. Your nachos will thank you. Your mashed potatoes—oh yes—they will thank you very, very much.

CORN PUDDING WITH CRÈME FRAÎCHE

I used to live near a Jamaican take-out joint called Gerry's in St. Clair West Village in Toronto. The family made what I thought was the best Jamaican food in the city. Pepper-pot soup, fish tea, amazing goat roti, perfect beef patties, and their corn "pone," which was to die for. I never had the chance to ask them for their recipe, but this one comes close enough to make me want to take a trip back up to my old neighbourhood.

SERVES 6

1 TEASPOON COCONUT OIL, FOR GREASING PAN
1 CUP CORNMEAL
1 CUP ALL-PURPOSE FLOUR
1/2 CUP DRIED SWEETENED COCONUT (SHREDDED)
1 TABLESPOON BAKING POWDER
1 TEASPOON SALT
1/4 TEASPOON GROUND NUTMEG
4 TABLESPOONS COCONUT OIL, MELTED
2 LARGE EGGS, BEATEN
2 TABLESPOONS UNSALTED BUTTER, MELTED
1 TABLESPOON HONEY
1 CUP WHOLE MILK
1 14-OUNCE (400 ML) CAN COCONUT MILK
1/2 CUP CONDENSED, SWEETENED COCONUT MILK
CRÈME FRAÎCHE, FOR SERVING
PINCH OF GROUND CINNAMON

PREHEAT YOUR OVEN to 350°F. Grease an 8- × 10-inch cake pan with coconut oil.

IN A BOWL, mix together corn meal, flour, coconut, baking powder, salt, and nutmeg. In a separate bowl, mix together coconut oil, eggs, butter, honey, milk, coconut milk, and condensed coconut milk. Add the dry mixture to the wet, blending until smooth and well combined.

POUR THE BATTER into the prepared cake pan and bake for 45 minutes, or until the edges begin to darken and the surface has hardened. The consistency should be like a very moist cake. If it's too much on the pudding side, continue baking for another 5 minutes.

SET ASIDE to cool on a baking rack until ready to serve. Serve with a scoop creme fraîche on top and a light dusting of cinnamon.

ACKNOWLEDGEMENTS

So many names come to mind over a lifetime of obsessing over beef steak, so I've settled on the very fine people who helped me give this book life: my astute editor, Brad Wilson, who was among the first to recognize and harness the power of my fascination; my agent, Samantha Haywood, for always being in my corner; my frequent partner-in-steak, Brad Jolly, for his never-ending encouragement, conversation, and guidance; my recipe editor, Tracy Bordian, without whom this book would have been tragically unintelligible; my butcher and friend, Peter Sanagan, for his inspiration, confidence, expertise, wonderful Foreword, and crucial advice, so freely given; the fine folks at Vince Gasparo's Meat Market and at Segovia Foods; proofreaders Shaun Oakey and Linda Pruessen, and champion indexer Ruth Pincoe; designer Lisa Bettencourt and art director Alan Jones, who made everything look as brilliant as possible; my conduit to the outside world, Ivy Knight, who told me this was worth it; my publisher, Iris Tupholme, for her faith in me; Sandra Leef, Michael Guy-Haddock, and everyone at HarperCollins; Mike McColl and Mia Bachmaier for contributing beautiful photos and food styling; my parents, for their support and encouragement; and my darling wife, Noelle Zitzer, who as an editor kept this book from falling off the shelf and as a friend kept me to sunny ways.

SOURCES

Blumenthal, Heston. *The Fat Duck Cookbook.* London: Cape Press, 2008.

Hahn Niman, Nicolette. *Defending Beef: The Case for Sustainable Meat Production.* White River Junction, VT: Chelsea Green Publishing, 2014.

Harvey, Graham. *Grass-Fed Nation: Getting Back the Food We Deserve.* London: Icon Books, 2016.

Hertzmann, Peter. *Knife Skills Illustrated: A User's Manual.* New York: W.W. Norton & Company, 2007.

Krasner, Deborah. *Good Meat: The Complete Guide to Sourcing and Cooking Sustainable Meat.* New York: Stewart, Tabori and Chang, 2010.

LaFrieda, Pat. *Meat: Everything You Need to Know.* New York: Atria Books, 2014.

López-Alt, J. Kenji. *The Food Lab: Better Home Cooking Through Science.* New York: W.W. Norton & Company, 2015.

Le, Stephen. *100 Million Years of Food: What Our Ancestors Ate and Why It Matters Today.* Toronto: HarperCollins, 2016.

McGee, Harold. *On Food and Cooking: The Science and Lore of the Kitchen.* New York: Scribner, 2004.

Mylan, Tom. *The Meat Hook Meat Book: Buy, Butcher, and Cook Your Way to Better Meat.* New York: Artisan, 2014.

Schatzker, Mark. *Steak: One Man's Search for the World's Tastiest Piece of Beef.* New York: Penguin Books, 2011.

Schwartz, Judith D. *Cows Save the Planet, and Other Improbable Ways of Restoring Soil to Heal the Earth.* White River Junction, VT: Chelsea Green Publishing, 2013.

Teicholz, Nina. *The Big Fat Surprise: Why Butter, Meat and Cheese Belong in a Healthy Diet.* New York: Simon & Schuster, 2014.

INDEX

ROB FIRING is well known to butchers around Toronto as a steak fanatic. He has written for *Publishers Weekly*, the *Toronto Star*, and various food blogs, and shares his food writing on www.MissionSteak.com. Rob is also the co-author (with Ivy Knight and Kerry Knight) of *The Everyday Squash Cook*, which was a finalist for a Taste Canada Award. As a publishing professional with over 20 years of expertise in cookbooks, he has worked with some of the biggest names in food in Canada and around the world, including Anthony Bourdain, Jamie Oliver, David Rocco, Laura Calder, and Jamie Kennedy. Rob lives in Toronto.